THE BIG BOOK OF GHOSTS

GYLES BRANDRETH
Illustrated by David Simonds

Carousel Books
Transworld Publishers Ltd.

Other books by Gyles Brandreth

1000 FACTS
1000 JOKES
1000 BLUNDERS
1000 SECRETS
1000 TONGUE-TWISTERS
1000 KNOCK-KNOCKS
1000 CRAZY RECORDS
THE BIG BOOK OF MAGIC
THE BIG BOOK OF SECRETS
THE BIG BOOK OF PRACTICAL JOKES
THE BIG BOOK OF USELESS INVENTIONS
THE CRAZY WORD BOOK
THE CRAZY ENCYCLOPAEDIA
THE CRAZY BOOK OF WORLD RECORDS
WHAT DO YOU KNOW?
CHALLENGE
DON'T YOU BELIEVE IT!

All published by Carousel Books

THE BIG BOOK OF GHOSTS

A CAROUSEL BOOK 0 552 54262 8

First published in Great Britain in 1984

PUBLISHING HISTORY
CAROUSEL edition published 1984

Carousel Books are published by
Transworld Publishers,
Century House
61-63 Uxbridge Road
Ealing, London W.5.

Printed and bound in Great Britain by
Cox & Wyman Ltd, Reading

Contents

THE BIG BOOK OF GHOSTS

Aaaah!

Here's a haunting question!

HAVE YOU EVER SEEN A GHOST?

The answer could be yes! Not all ghosts are in Elizabethan dress with their heads tucked underneath their arms. Ghosts can often look so normal that you can walk past one in the street and never even realise. That little girl coming out of the sweetshop, an old lady crossing the road, a tramp sitting outside the library — they may look real enough, but seeing isn't always believing. They **could** be ghosts.

So, what is a ghost? The word '**ghost**' means **any kind of apparition**, from 'white ladies' that float through walls, the faint smell of gun-powder that can suddenly appear on a battlefield two-hundred years after the battle, to the sound of clinking chains from an age gone by. They all have one thing in common — they are uncanny events that nobody can explain.

In this book you can glimpse the strange world of the supernatural and discover screaming skulls, headless monks, haunted houses to visit, creepy castles to avoid, bloodstained floorboards that will never dry, and phantom figures that will never die. Walk with me into the unknown — it could make your flesh creep, your blood chill, your hair stand on end, and your hands go clammy. . . . and if you've never seen a ghost, this could be your chance!

Boys and Ghouls

Boys and ghouls come out to play. . . . to help you enter into the spirit of this book, here are some ghostly games for you to play with your friends.

BONES

Find a picture of a skeleton in a magazine and cut it up, preferably into bones — but you can cut it into pieces like a jig-saw if you wish. Divide the bones amongst the players so that each has an equal number. You must then take it in turn to lay down a bone, but you must only lay a bone that will join on to the skeleton. For example, if the skeleton is being built from the skull downwards and you only seem to have bones of the leg and feet, then you must miss a go until you can join a bone on.

Take it in turns to lay a bone, and the player that lays the final bone and completes the skeleton is the winner!

GROANS

For this game you can have any number of players. Blindfold one player and sit him or her on the ground. When the person is seated the rest of the players sit around in a circle, with the blindfolded player in the middle who will have no idea in which order you are sitting. Each player in turn must then make a ghostly groan or eerie wail, and the blindfolded person must guess who is making the groan. Each player must take it in turns to be blindfolded and the one that identifies the most groans is the winner.

GHOSTS

For this game you will need a large white sheet and at least four players. Before you begin the game each player must remove his or her shoes and socks. One player must then leave the room, during which time the remaining players get under the sheet so that only their feet are sticking out. The object of the game is for the player who left the room to return and identify the 'ghost's' feet sticking out from under the sheet.

The ghosts can hide under the sheet in **TWO** ways. They can either all lie on the floor in a row with their feet sticking out **OR**, which is much more fun, they can all stand together in a group and place the sheet over the top of themselves so that they look like one big ghost with many feet. They must then try and jumble their feet up so that it is impossible to see which are paired together. The player who left the room must then return with as many pieces of ribbon as there are players under the sheet and begin to tie a piece of ribbon around **ONE** ankle of each person. He or she will see perhaps eight or ten feet under the sheet, all jumbled up, and must tie ribbons to four or five of the ankles. If this player is really clever, when the ghosts emerge from the sheet each will have a ribbon tied around one ankle. If the player has not paired the feet up correctly one person will have a piece of ribbon around both ankles and somebody will have none.

MURDER

This gruesome game is ideal for a party, but is only for those with nerves of steel. You will need to prepare for this game beforehand, and you'll see why in a minute. What you are going to do is sit everybody in a circle and tell them a ghost story. You put out all the lights so that the room is in pitch blackness. Then you begin your story.

You tell the story of a gruesome murder. Say that the murderer began by gouging out the eyes of his victim. You then pass around the circle two large peeled grapes! When they have passed around the circle and back to you, you can continue your story.

Next, you say, the murderer cut off the top of the victim's skull and scooped out the brains. You then pass around a wet sponge. Use your imagination to continue the story and pass around suitable items. An ear can be a small cabbage leaf, carrots can be fingers, a piece of potato can be a nose, and so on.

In each case wait until the item has been passed round every member of the circle and returned to you before continuing with your story.

TOMBS

You will need three players for this game. The idea being that two people have been trapped in a tomb by a terrible monster-like ghost. Only one person has the chance to escape. One player becomes the ghost of the tomb, the other two are blindfolded.

The player who is the ghost then moans in a loud voice:

*'Mortal men your time has come,
Find the keys or die.'*

and throws a bunch of keys on the ground.

The two blindfolded players must listen very carefully to where the keys are dropped and then begin to search for them. The first player to find the keys is spared and escapes from the tomb, scoring one point. The other player then goes on to become the monster.

HAUNTS

This is a memory game that any number of ghosts can play. All the players must sit round in a circle, preferably in a darkened room with a candle in the middle of the circle. The **first** player then says:

'I am the ghost that walks the night and I have haunted Hever Castle.'

The **second** player must continue:

'I am the ghost that walks the night and I have haunted Hever Castle and Marple Hall.'

Each player in turn adds a haunt. If anyone forgets a haunt they drop out of the circle. The winner is the last one left.

Castles With Ghosts

ARUNDEL CASTLE, Sussex.

This impressive castle is now open to the public for part of the year, so you can go along and ghost hunt for yourself. There are at least three known ghosts here. A blue Cavalier, a kitchen maid who committed suicide in the kitchen, and a young girl who having lost her love threw herself from one of the towers.

BERRY POMEROY CASTLE, Devon.

This ruined castle is haunted by the spectre of Lady Margaret Pomeroy. She beckons to travellers and lures them into her tower, where they then mysteriously fall to their death.

BRAMBER CASTLE, Sussex.

Over eight hundred years ago the children of William de Breone (then owner of the castle) were captured by King John and were held hostage. Eventually the children starved to death, and today their pitiful ghosts haunt the castle grounds begging for food.

DOVER CASTLE, Kent.

If you visit this castle and hear the sound of eerie drumming, it will only be a headless drummer boy who had his head chopped off during the Napoleonic wars.

FEATHERSTONE CASTLE, Northumberland.

Haunted by the ghost of Sir Reginald FitzUrse who was locked up and starved to death in one of the towers. His ghostly groans and clanking of his armour continue to be heard.

FYVIE CASTLE, Aberdeenshire.

One of the most horribly haunted castles in the country, with curses, bloodstains that will never wash away, and a ghost, part of the castle has been closed for ever because something dreadful happens to anyone who enters.

GLAMIS CASTLE, Angus.

This former home of Queen Elizabeth, the Queen Mother, and birthplace of Princess Margaret, has over 100 rooms, one of which has a secret chamber which nobody ever enters. It contains a horrible monster that is strangely kept alive. One of the Earls of Strathmore once said:

'If you could only guess the nature of the secret, you would go down on your knees and thank God it was not yours.'

Other Glamis ghosts include the Earl of Baerdie who has to play cards eternally, having lost his soul to the Devil in a card game — he now tries to win it back.

HASTINGS CASTLE, Sussex.

Now just a ruin, the castle is still visited by the spectre of Thomas à Becket on Autumn evenings and the sounds of rattling chains and pitiful groans have been heard too.

HERSTMONCEUX CASTLE, Sussex.

Centuries ago an elderly Lord Dacre married a beautiful young girl. Determined to keep her, he used to play the drum to frighten everyone away so that she met nobody else. Tired of being alone with the old man she locked him in a room and left him there to die. His ghostly drumming can still be heard.

HYLTON CASTLE, Yorkshire.

Roger Skelton, a stableboy who was murdered in 1609, has turned into a mischievous ghost known as the '*Cauld Lad of Hylton*' who turns things upside-down when he gets the chance!

INVERARAY CASTLE, Wigtownshire.

A ghostly harper who was hanged in the castle can be heard on the stairs and in the library. It is also said that when a death of the Chief of the Clan is going to happen, a ghostly galleon passes up the loch past the castle.

LYMPNE CASTLE, Kent.

During Roman times a soldier fell to his death from a tower and has haunted the castle ever since. There are also the ghosts of six Saxons who were slaughtered here during the Norman invasion.

PENGERSICK CASTLE, Cornwall.

Pengersick can boast two ghosts. The first is a Tudor ghost called Mr. Millington who purchased the castle during the reign of King Henry VIII. He tried to murder his wife with a goblet of poisoned wine, but the shrewd wife swopped the drinks over and the would-be murderer drank his own poison!

The second ghost is that of a wicked baron who threw his wife and son into the sea. The boy was saved by a passing ship, but the wife was drowned. Her spirit entered into the body of a white hare and it is said that the baron was killed when he was thrown from his horse. The horse shied at. . . . a white hare. The baron's ghost still haunts the castle.

SCOTNEY CASTLE, Kent.

In the eighteenth century the owner of Scotney, one Arthur Darrell, was killed abroad and brought home for burial. His ghost was later seen standing by the graveside and uttering the words, '*That is not me.*' In 1920 the grave was opened and the coffin was found to be full of stones. Darrell still haunts the castle. Is he searching for his body?

TAUNTON CASTLE, SOMERSET.

A bedroom in the castle is haunted by the wicked Judge Jefferies, known as the 'Hanging Judge' because of the terrible punishments he inflicted on his victims.

Visitors to the bedroom have felt a pair of unseen hands around their throat and the sound of a ghostly violin plays haunting melodies.

THE TOWER OF LONDON.

The scene of many bloody happenings it is quite naturally the haunt of a number of spectres. The ghosts of the two Princes murdered in the Tower, the spectre of Anne Boleyn minus her head, Lord Northumberland, the beheaded Lady Salisbury, and a bear are just some of the apparitions that appear. The most recent ghost to be seen was that of Lady Jane Grey who appears on the anniversary of her death, 12 February.

VERDLEY CASTLE, Sussex.

Ghosts aren't always in human form, and one of the strangest ghosts appears at Verdley — that of a bear. It is said to be the spirit of the very last wild bear to be killed in England.

WARDOUR CASTLE, Wiltshire.

Blanche, Lady Arundel, haunts the castle grounds and can be seen standing beside the lake at twilight. The appearance of a white owl foretells the death of one of the Arundel family.

WINDSOR CASTLE, Berkshire.

Apart from being haunted by the spectres of Queen Elizabeth I and George III, as discussed later in this book, the park is haunted by the dreadful Herne the Hunter. The spectral hunter and his pack of hounds appears in deerskin clothes with antlers on his head and riding a horse breathing fire. Herne has haunted the forest since the time of Richard II, and is reputed to have appeared before Henry VIII while riding through the royal park.

WOODCROFT CASTLE, Huntingdonshire.

Haunted by the ghost of a Dr. Hudson, who was chaplain to King Charles I. After Charles had been beheaded the doctor was thrown over the castle battlements by the Roundheads. He clung to the castle walls, where they promptly chopped off his hands and he fell to his death.

Dressing the Part

Whether it's Hallowe'en, a fancy dress party, or simply a time when you want to surprise your friends, why not dress up as a ghost? Here are some creepy costume ideas.

TRADITIONAL GHOST

The traditional ghost costume is still one of the most effective, especially when seen in a dimly lit room. All you need is one plain white sheet with two small eye holes cut in it so that you can see where you are going. Drape the sheet over your head, with your arms raised in the air in a haunting position and you will be ready to scare anyone you might meet.

To make your ghost costume even more frightening, use a black felt-tip pen to draw a grinning skull face on the sheet, and you will look like a skeleton in a shroud.

THE WHITE LADY

To become a phantom white lady you will need a long white dress (or a white sheet draped around you will do) and some white gloves, some talcum powder, and a stick of white theatrical make-up. Begin by covering your face with white make-up so that you look deathly pale. Dab some talcum powder into your hair so that it looks white. Now wear all white clothes, and your costume is complete.

HORROR HEADS

For a simple, but very effective, costume that would be ideal for a fancy dress party all you need is a small cardboard box. Choose one that fits neatly over your head. Cut out some eye holes, and a hole for the mouth on **each** side of the box. This is so that you can breathe and see where you are going. Now you can have great fun with paints, felt-tip pens, pieces of string, wool, coloured paper, in fact anything you like to create four different horror faces — one on each side of the box. Depending upon which way you wear the box, you have four horror masks.

WICKED WITCH

1. To create a witch's hat, begin by cutting a circle of card about 30cm square. Draw a circle the same size as your head in the centre of this circle and then one slightly smaller than your head. Cut out the smallest circle and then bend the card upwards on the next circle line, which will give you a tab all around on which to glue the top of the hat:

I

II

III

2. Next cut a circle 60cm in diameter. Make a cut from one edge to the centre and slide it around to form a cone. Glue this to the brim of your hat, and it is finished. Use black card if you can, but if not you can paint it black.

3. Around the inside edge of the hat, glue some lengths of string or wool at the back and sides to look like long witch's hair. Wear the hat with a black cloak around you and the costume is almost complete.

4. To finish off the costume, get some old flesh coloured rubber gloves and glue some long pointed cardboard nails at the ends and you will have some ugly hands. Now you can go and make some spells.

Why do witches ride a broomstick?

Because a vacuum cleaner is too heavy!

VAMPIRE

Vampires all look rather like the evil Count Dracula, and live by drinking fresh blood every night. To give yourself vampire-like teeth, cut a shape like this out of white shiny card:

When placed under your top lip they will look just like real fangs. Decorate the ends with a non-toxic red felt-tip pen to look like dripping blood. Dip a comb in water and smooth your hair back off your face, a black cloak draped around your shoulders will add the finishing touch.

ZOMBIE

A zombie is a dead body that has been brought back to life. They cannot speak and stare horribly. To make yourself look like a zombie, comb your hair right back off your face. Then cover your face with white make-up and dab on some talcum powder, so that your skin looks dry and corpse-like. Use grey eyeshadow to put dark rings around your eyes, and put a little just under your cheek bones to give your face a thin, hollow look. Wear old clothes so that you look as if you have just crawled out of the grave, and practise your zombie-like stare so that you really do look like the walking dead.

Eerie Noises

Not all ghosts appear as white ladies or as headless knights. Some make their presence felt in other ways — by making a noise. The most frightening noise of all is that of a banshee, an unseen creature whose mournful cry foretells a death. It is said to be like the howling of cats that gets louder and louder, and yet there is something strangely human about the cry.

Other eerie noises come from the skulls of long dead relatives, that are said to scream when removed from their final resting place. Here are some stories of ghostly noises. . . .

FATHER AMBROSE

If you ever visit Wardley Hall in Manchester, you will see in a small recess at the top of the stairs a skull. It is that of Father Ambrose, a Catholic monk who was hanged in 1641. If anyone tries to remove his skull from the Hall, a terrible howling wind starts to rage and weird noises echo through the house.

On one occasion a new housemaid started work at Wardley Hall, and on seeing the gruesome skull she threw it into the moat. An incredible storm started, with wind howling and rain lashing, which continued until the skull was fished out of the moat and returned to the house.

THE BETTISCOMBE SKULL

In 1767 a West Indian Slave, known as 'Old Bettiscombe' was brought to England to work for the owner of Bettiscombe Manor in Dorset, Azariah Pinney, where he worked until his death. The slave was treated very well, and was promised by his master that when he died his body would be taken back to the West Indies. Pinney did not keep his promise and when the slave died he was simply buried in the local churchyard. From that time onwards strange things happened at the Manor. Screams and cries were heard in the night, there were ghostly groans and mysterious crashing noises. It became so bad that eventually the body was dug up and the skull was brought back to the Manor. The noises stopped.

On any occasion since, if anyone has tried to remove the skull it is said to scream *'like a trapped rat'*, there are terrible thunderstorms, and the person who removes the skull always dies within a year. The present owner of the Manor makes sure that the skull stays in the house, for obvious reasons!

One final point about the Bettiscombe skull that nobody can explain. On the eve of the First World War the skull sweated blood . . .

WILLIAM CORDER

In April 1828 William Corder, aged 23, was hanged for murder. William's skeleton was taken to West Suffolk Hospital where it was used to educate students, so that they could see what human bones were like. A Dr. John Kilner at the hospital collected skulls as a hobby and so had his eye on William's. One night he stole it and took it home. That night his bedroom was filled with the sounds of somebody sobbing, ghostly breathing, and a restless spirit seemed to walk the room. The doctor was so frightened that he returned the skull, and the noises stopped.

THE OGILVY CLAN

Centuries ago at Glamis Castle, Angus, there was a feud between two rival Scottish clans, the Ogilvys and the Lindsays. Seeking refuge the Ogilvys went to Glamis Castle where the Earl of Strathmore hid them in a room. He was, however, in sympathy with the Lindsays and left the Ogilvys there to starve. The men died horribly by gnawing themselves to death, and their ghostly screams can be heard in one part of the castle.

ANNE GRIFFITH

In 1590 Anne Griffith built a beautiful house in Yorkshire, known as Burton Agnes Hall. Anne loved the house, but shortly after it was completed she was out walking one day when she was attacked by robbers and left mortally injured. On her death bed Anne requested that when she died, she wanted her head cut off and kept in the house.

After her death, her sisters thought that this wish was much too gruesome to carry out and so they buried Anne, complete with head. Within a short time horrendous noises occurred in the middle of the night, ghostly footsteps could be heard, doors slammed, and eventually the noises got so bad that the sisters were forced to have Anne's coffin opened. When they did so they discovered that although her recently buried body was intact, her head was separate from the body and had already become a skull. This was brought to the house and immediately the noises stopped. If anyone has ever tried to remove the skull, it has started to scream and the hauntings have begun. In 1900 the skull was bricked into one of the walls so that it will remain there as long as Burton Agnes Hall, and '*Awd Nance*', as the skull is known, seems to be happy.

Frightening Faces!

Here are some of the more frightening ghosts you might encounter. . . . .

ANNIE

'Wandsworth Annie', as she is known, haunts the Victorian jail at Wandsworth. An ugly, toothless spectre, dressed in a morbid grey prison uniform is seen to glide slowly through the corridors.

FATHER BENEDICTUS

In 1303 Father Benedictus was murdered by thieves in the cloisters of Westminster Abbey. Today the phantom monk walks through the cloisters each evening at five o'clock. He is said to be tall, with a hooked nose, and very penetrating eyes.

MOTHER BARNES

In 1575, at Littlecote Manor, Wiltshire, Mother Barnes became witness to a particularly gruesome and grisly murder. She was asked to go to the Manor by '*wicked*' Will Darrell, where his son was being born. Mother Barnes helped with the birth, whereupon Darrell immediately picked up the baby and threw it on the fire. She was threatened with death if she ever told anyone. Today her pathetic ghost is seen kneeling by the fireside. The ghosts of mother and baby have also been seen.

TOM BUSBY

In 1702 Tom Busby was hanged for the murder of his father-in-law. He now haunts the Busby Stoop Inn, Sandhutton, North Yorkshire, where a chair is kept for him. The ghost has a lolling head, a swollen tongue, and the hangman's noose still around his neck.

JOHN BREED

An eighteenth century butcher, John Breed committed cold blooded murder by stabbing a man in the back with his butcher's cleaver in St. Mary's Churchyard, 1743. His skull is kept in Rye Town Hall, and his fearsome spectre still walks the churchyard.

LADY CAMPBELL

In 1807 at Coombe Bank in Kent, Lady Campbell was burned to death, having been cursed by her first husband. All that remained of her was a small piece of her thumb. Her ghost, minus one thumb, continues to search for the missing piece.

CAVALIERS

Since the Battle of Marston Moor in 1644, in which more than four thousand men were killed, the blood-stained spectres of Cavaliers have been witnessed walking along a road through the battlefield.

PIEMAN CLIBBON

Pieman Clibbon was an eighteenth century market trader, selling pies in the market place at Datchworth, Hertfordshire. On the way home from market he would disguise himself and rob one of the other traders of his days takings. When he was eventually discovered, Clibbon was tied to a horse and dragged along the road until he died. His roped body can be seen in spectral form around the Datchworth Lanes, and his deathly screams can be heard.

LADY EDITHA

A particularly ghastly nun, known as Lady Editha, haunts Tamworth Castle in Staffordshire. She climbs up the spiral stairs of one of the towers and moans pitifully. Her ghostly cries have even been tape recorded.

SIR WALTER GIFFORD

At midnight the ghost of a phantom knight glides through the churchyard at Weare Gifford in Devon. His spooky raps on the church door can be heard and the eerie creaks as the door swings open and the ghost disappears.

HAIRY HANDS

At a point on Dartmoor, two horrible hairy hands have been known to appear in thin air and grab hold of the steering wheels of cars or the handle bars of motor cyclists, causing serious and fatal accidents.

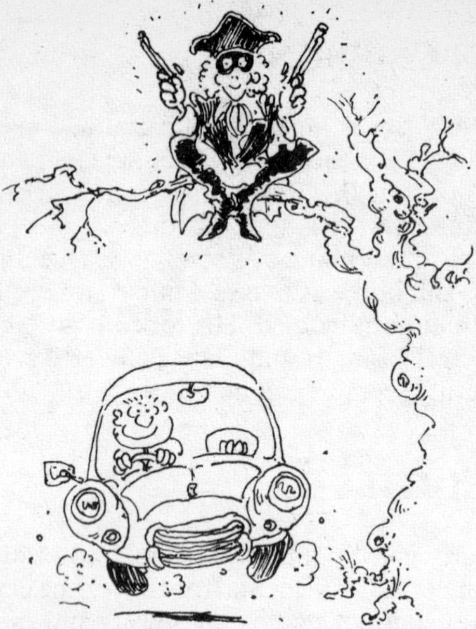

KATHERINE FERRERS

Longing for excitement in life, Katherine dressed as a man and became a highwayman. She would climb up trees and jump on people that passed below and rob them. One night she was shot by one of her victims and so became a victim herself. On moonless nights her ghost still lies in wait for unsuspecting people.

BROTHER JOSEPH

Each year the ugly spectre of a hunchbacked monk makes a pilgrimage from Buckfast Abbey in Devon to the sea. Not a person you would like to meet!

ELIZABETH PATEMAN

The ruins of Moco Farm, near Cambridge, are haunted by the grisly ghost of nineteen year old Elizabeth who was stabbed to death in 1750 and still cries out in pain and fear.

SEVERED ARM

Never accept an invitation to stay at Capesthorne Hall in Cheshire! People who have slept there have woken in the middle of the night to find a chopped off arm climbing across the bedclothes towards them. Yuk!

SIR THOMAS VAUGHAN

In 1843 Sir Thomas was beheaded. His former home, Hergerst Hall in Herefordshire, is now said to be haunted by his head which hovers around on its own.

PHANTOM VIOLINIST

As the *Titanic* sank in April 1912, the orchestra played '*Nearer My God to Thee*'. One of the violinists survived, although he never played again. He sold the violin to a Mr. Culver, and the ghostly spirit of the phantom fiddler has since been heard playing the haunting melody.

WIDOW LEAKY

Known as the **'Whistling Spectre'**, Widow Leaky walks down the streets of Minehead in Somerset, making a spine chilling whistle as she goes, that causes the hair of anyone that hears her to stand on end.

Ghostly Giggles

Why are vampires mad?

Because they're often bats.

What kind of music do ghosts like?

Something with a haunting melody.

What do you call ghostly twins that keep ringing bells?

Dead ringers.

At a Ghost School a teacher was showing young ghouls how to walk through walls. *'Do you see how it's done?'* **she asked,** *'Just to make sure, I'll go through it again.'*

'I feel half dead.'
'We'll arrange for you to be buried up to your waist.'

What do ghosts eat for supper?

Ghoulash.

Who looks after ghosts in a phantom football team?

The Ghoul Keeper.

What are a ghoul's best friend?

Demons.

What do ghosts play at birthday parties?

Haunt and seek.

What do ghouls eat with meat?

Grave-y.

What do you flatten a ghost with?

A spirit level.

What is a ghost's unfavourite motto?

Never say die.

What do ghosts eat for breakfast?

Dreaded wheat.

Did you hear about the stupid ghost?

It climbed over a wall.

Where do ghosts go at Christmas?

To the phantomime.

How do ghosts keep their feet dry?

By wearing boo-oots.

What advice did the mother ghost give her baby ghost?

Only spook when you're spooken to.

Why did the teacher always give the ghost bad marks?

Because he kept making a ghoul of himself.

What did the barman say to the ghost?

'I'm sorry, but we don't serve spirits.'

What do short-sighted ghosts wear?

Spooktacles.

What do you call a drunk ghost?

A methylated spirit.

What did the baby ghost say when he wanted his favourite food?

'I Scream!'

Why do ghosts like tall buildings?

Because they have a lot of scarecases.

What happens when a man ghost meets a lady ghost?

It's love at first fright.

Who saves a ghost if he falls into the sea?

The Ghost guard.

What do ghosts take for a cough?

Coffin drops.

What did the mummy ghost say to the baby ghost?

'Don't eat with your fingers, use your shovel.'

What do you get when you have your head chopped off?

A splitting headache.

Why aren't ghosts good liars?

Because you can see right through them.

What should you do if a ghost floated in through your front door?

Run out of your back door!

What do you get if you cross a ghost with a packet of crisps?

Snacks that go crunch in the night.

Where do ghosts get their jokes from?

Crypt writers.

What kind of mistake does a ghost make?

A boo-boo.

Where do ghosts live?

In a far off terrortory.

What do ghostly soldiers say to strangers?

'Who ghost there?'

How do ghosts get through a locked door?

With a skeleton key?

Can a vampire with no teeth still bite you?

No, but he can give you a very nasty suck.

Which jewels do ghosts like wearing best?

Tomb stones.

Where does a Red Indian's ghost live?

In a creepy teepee.

Haunted Houses

. . . . . the top haunted houses in Britain.

ALTHORP HOUSE, Northamptonshire.

The home of Earl and Countess Spencer, father and stepmother of the Princess of Wales, is fortunately haunted by a very friendly ghost. It is said to be that of an old and faithful servant, who visits any room at night that has a light left on. The ghost is only concerned that someone might have fallen asleep leaving a candle burning.

ATHELHAMPTON HALL, Dorset.

The only house on record to be haunted by a spectral monkey, which was a pet of the Martyn family who lived at the Hall in 1595. Other ghosts include a Grey Lady who simply fades away if you approach her; a Black Priest who is seen in broad daylight outside the bathroom; a Phantom Cooper who hammers away at wine barrels in the cellar, and two ghostly swordsmen who fight a duel in the Great Chamber. All have been seen in recent years.

BISHAM ABBEY, Berkshire.

Poor young William Hoby hated studying and when he made a mess of one of his exercise books, his mother, Lady Elizabeth Hoby beat him to death. It is her ghost that sobs hysterically as it glides through the house. In front of her is always a bowl of water in which she eternally attempts to wash the blood from her hands.

BORLEY RECTORY, Essex.

Now destroyed by fire, it was once said to be the most haunted house in Britain. It was haunted by a ghostly nun, a phantom coach, the Rev. Henry Bull (builder of the rectory), and a whole host of strange phenomena such as ringing bells, the door bell always rang during violent storms, all kind of objects flew around the rooms, and even ghostly messages appeared on the walls. In 1939 the house unaccountably burnt to the ground, and human remains believed to be those of the ghostly nun were found when the ruins were eventually demolished.

THE BLACK HOUSE, Brixham.

In the house the ghost of Squire Hilliard, a former occupant, makes his presence felt. Over 400 years ago his son fell in love with a girl, but the Squire did not approve of the match and forced the girl to marry somebody else. The son went off and hanged himself. Now the ghost of Squire Hilliard searches for his son to beg forgiveness.

CAMFIELD PLACE, Hertfordshire.

Once the home of writer Beatrix Potter, now the home of romantic novelist, Barbara Cartland. The former once saw a hand put out twelve candles one by one.

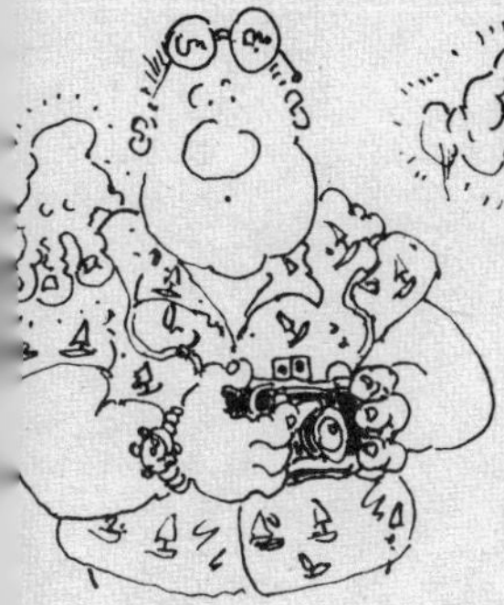

CHINGLE HALL, Lancashire.

This moated manor house, built in 1260, is haunted by two monks, a priest, ghostly footsteps, doors open and close on their own, and a pair of ghostly hands guide visitors to the drawing room.

HOLLAND HOUSE, London.

Before being bombed during the war, one of the rooms in this house contained a recess in which there were three bloodstains that could not be removed.

The bloodstains marked the place where the ghost of Lord Holland would appear, holding his head in his hands. Although the house has gone, the ghost has not.

LANGLEY HALL, Durham.

At midnight a ghostly hearse pulls up at the house, drawn by headless horses and with a headless coachman. Whose body have they come to collect?

LEWTRENCHARD HOUSE,
Dartmoor.

Footsteps in the night and the sound of unseen carriage wheels coming down the drive here appear to be connected with an eighteenth-century inhabitant, Mrs. Baring-Gould. If anyone tries to see where the sounds are coming from, peels of maniacal laughter ring out through the night.

LONGLEAT, Wiltshire.

One of England's greatest stately homes, of course has a number of ghosts, including one that knocks on bedroom doors in the middle of the night. There is also a Green Lady, which is probably the ghost of Lady Louise Carteret who murdered her husband and hid his body under the cellar floor. His skeleton was discovered in recent years.

PURSE CAUNDLE MANOR,
Somerset.

This former hunting lodge is visited by King John's hounds on Midsummer's Eve. A phantom huntsman's horn and the sound of baying hounds can be heard, although nobody has ever seen them. Also the chanting of plainsong by ghostly monks can occasionally be heard.

SALISBURY HOUSE, Hertfordshire.

For many years the ghost of a Cavalier with a sword through his body, and a number of other ghosts used to walk through the wall in a bedroom. When alterations were made to the house it was discovered that in this exact spot was a doorway that had been bricked up.

SAWSTON HALL, Cambridgeshire.

The ghost of Mary Tudor, known as **'Bloody Mary'** is thought to haunt the Tapestry Room and the sound of a spinet is heard. People who sleep in a bedroom in which Mary slept say that the latch of the door is lifted by unseen hands.

THURSTASTON HALL, Cheshire.

Although nobody knows who she is, the ghost of an old lady wringing her hands in despair is said to appear **every night**.

WOLFETON HOUSE, Dorset.

This five hundred year old house is haunted by two of its former occupants. One drives up in a phantom coach pulled by a pair of horses, the second is a headless grey lady who appears in the Great Chamber.

WYCOLLER HALL, Lancashire.

This is the house that Charlotte Brontë used in her novel *Jane Eyre* as Ferndean Manor. Now a ruin, it is still haunted by a spectral horserider who rides up to the house. This is followed by screaming and deathly groans.

ZEALS HOUSE, Wiltshire.

Yet another Grey Lady, who walks down the stairs through the house and out into the woods. At the spot to which she walks is a stone. This marks the place where a female skeleton was found. The Grey Lady's?

I Spy

Would you like to be a ghost hunter? There have been ghosts for thousands and thousands of years, we know that they exist, but nobody has ever been able to **prove** it. Although there are professional ghost hunters who have special electronic equipment that helps them detect falls in temperature (a room goes icy cold when a ghost is present), and spend their lives sleeping in haunted houses — they probably frighten ghosts away with their elaborate traps.

With a few pieces of simple equipment, you can become a ghost hunter. Here's what you will need:

NOTEBOOK

If you think that a particular room, perhaps of your house, is haunted then keep a notebook to write down all the details you can about your ghost. Try and find out if anybody has seen it, what it looks like, what times and dates it has appeared, and whose ghost it might be. Keep a note, too, of your experiences when you try to hunt down the ghost.

THERMOMETER

As the temperature drops when a ghost enters a room, a thermometer will help you detect any sudden temperature fall. Try and get a big one with easy to read markings.

RED LIGHT BULB

In the room in which you are going to wait for the ghost, put a red light bulb in the lamp and have that on as the only light. This will keep the room fairly dark, but you will still be able to see. It is also thought that ghosts are attracted to red light.

BLACK COTTON

Put a piece of cotton across the doors to the room. If your ghost turns out to be a fake and it is just somebody dressed up, they will break the cotton. A real ghost will pass through the door and the cotton without breaking it.

STICKY TAPE

A piece of sticky tape around the windows and doors will again ensure that nobody can try and fool you into thinking that something ghostly is happening by slipping something through the side of the door.

CAMERA

If you do see a ghost, then you want to be able to get evidence of it. What better proof than a photograph!

TAPE RECORDER

A tape recorder that can be left on in the room will record any sounds of the supernatural. On occasions people have recorded the sounds from a haunted room and have been able to hear actual voices when they played the tape back, even though they couldn't hear anything themselves.

A FRIEND

On a serious ghost hunt you need to have a friend with you. Not only will this stop you getting lonely or frightened, but it is important to have a witness with you. If at least two of you have seen the ghost it will prove that you haven't simply dreamed the ghost's appearance!

TAPE MEASURE

A tape measure will help you tell if anything in the room has been moved by supernatural forces. Teenager Conroy Winter from Birmingham one night put a glass on the table and it visibly moved across in front of his eyes. One night he awoke during the early hours of the morning to see a white figure sitting in a chair beside his bed. When he switched on the light the figure disappeared. If Conroy had kept his ghost hunting equipment with him, he perhaps could have managed to get a photograph of his ghost.

WHAT TO DO

Find out the most likely time and date that your ghost will appear. Anniversaries of deaths are usually the most promising times, as you will see from the diary at the end of the book.

Prepare the room in advance by setting up the tape-recorder and positioning your thermometer, camera, and so on. Make sure that the room is warm and that you have plenty of blankets too.

Settle yourselves in the room some time before the ghost is said to walk. It's no good arriving in the room at five minutes to twelve if the ghost always appears at midnight. Once inside, position the tape and the cotton. If objects have been known to move in the past, then chalk around the most likely objects so that you can measure the distance moved if something strange should happen. With the room lit by a single small red lamp, sit back calmly and wait for the ghost to appear.

Don't be disappointed if you see nothing the first time that you try it. Ghosts are unpredictable, sometimes they like to give proof that they exist, but tend not to appear if people seem to be watching for them. French photographer Samedi Soir once sat for one and a half hours in a room where a poltergeist was said to be. Suddenly, when he least expected it, a saucepan, a pair of scissors, and a letter rose into the air. He captured the happening on film, and laboratory tests prove that his photographs are not faked.

Happy hunting!

Just Joking

Have some spooky fun with your family and friends by playing a few ghostly tricks on them! **DON'T** play them on anybody very young, very nervous, or very frail, as you could really frighten them. You are, after all, just joking!

LEVITATION

When something **levitates it rises into the air all by itself without any visible means of support**. You can surprise visitors to your house by making something mysteriously rise, even when you are on the opposite side of the room.

1. Have a look in the needlework basket at home and see if there is any invisible thread. This is used for mending and although it is extremely strong, it is practically colourless and a single thread is like a very fine hair.

2. Next choose a very light object, such as a letter, a pencil, or a small book and attach the invisible thread to it, either with a piece of sticky tape or by tying it on.

3. Prepare your object before anybody else comes into the room. Lay the object on the floor or on a chair and drape the thread from something above it, by hanging it over the chair back or from some other object. Then trail the thread around the outside of the room to the opposite side where YOU will be sitting.

4. When someone comes into the room you can sit and talk quite naturally for five or ten minutes, then slowly pull on the thread without anyone noticing. Their eyes will be on the object on the opposite side of the room that is spookily rising into the air on the other side of the room! It can't be anything to do with you, because you are metres away!

GHOSTS IN THE NIGHT

If you want your parents to think that there is a real ghost in the house, all you need is a reel of cotton and an ordinary sheet of paper.

Just before your parents go to bed at night you can prepare this practical joke.

1. With a piece of adhesive tape, attach the cotton to the sheet of paper, and lay the piece of paper on top of their wardrobe where it is out of sight.

2. Trail the cotton down behind the wardrobe, along the skirting board, under the door and into your own bedroom. When your parents go into their room they will not notice anything at all. Allow them ten minutes to get into bed, or wait and see when their light goes out.

3. When all is silent, start to make low wailing noises like a demented ghost, and at the same time give your piece of cotton a very gentle tug. This will cause the piece of paper to float down off the top of the wardrobe, making an eerie rustling noise as it lands on the bed. Your parents will disappear under the bedcovers with fright and won't dare come out to investigate. If they do, well, you'll just be tucked up in bed, apparently fast asleep!

BLOOD BATH

When you are feeling particularly kind, tell your mother that you will run her a nice hot bath. Say that you think it's time she started to relax more.

1. You go into the bathroom and run the water and get the towels ready, the soap, the bathsalts and so on.

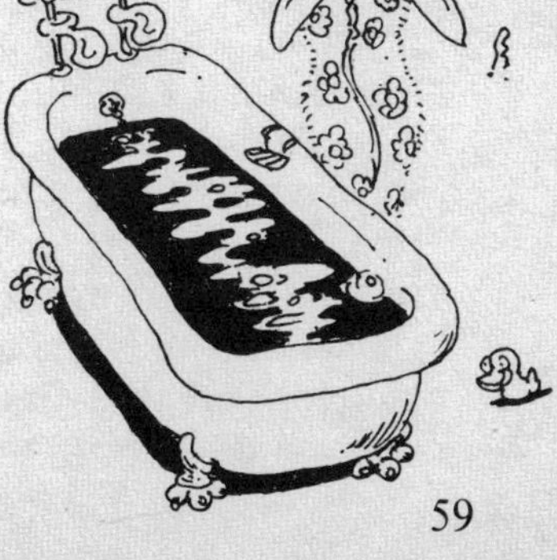

2. When the bath is ready, give her a call then run and hide. She will walk into the bathroom and you will hear: 'Aaaaaaaaaaggggggghhhhhhhh! Screeeeeaaaaaammmmm!'

3. The bath will look as if it is full of blood. You have put just a few drops of red food colouring or cochineal in the water. All you need are a couple of drops and the water will go blood red.

GHOSTS ALIVE!

Earlier in this book you will find some ideas for dressing up as a ghost. Dress up in secret and scare your family in the night. Everyone expects to see ghosts on Hallowe'en, 31 October, so if you do it then nobody will be frightened — but try it on 14 May, 5 April or 3 December and you **will** frighten people!

SPOOKY SOUNDS

People always hope that they will see a ghost one day, but how would they really react if they suddenly heard ghostly moans in the night or the clanking of chains?

1. If you have a tape recorder you can find out. Take a tape that is 120 minutes long, that is an hour each side. On one side wind the tape on to about halfway so that the first half an hour is blank. On the remainder of the tape, record a few ghastly noises. Moan like a demented spirit. Rattle a piece of chain. Record some ghostly footsteps or an ear-piercing scream — anything that sounds out of this world.

2. Once you have made your recording you can use it in a number of ways. Just as your friends arrive, hide the tape recorder in the room and switch it on. Remember that the first half an hour is blank, so there will be no sound. When your friends have arrived and settled down, turn the conversation to ghosts. You could even say that your own house is supposed to be haunted, and start to tell your friends about the ghost that roams your house, perhaps a grey lady who is searching for something, a headless knight who clanks around, or a shapeless hooded figure.

3. Just when your friends are starting to feel scared, without warning eerie ghostly sounds will start. Obviously they will have nothing to do with you because you've been sitting still for half an hour and haven't moved! If you look scared too it will appear even more realistic!

4. Another way is to put the tape on just as you are going out and the rest of the family are left alone in the house. You will be kilometres away before the noises start.

Kingly Ghosts

KING ARTHUR

Probably more legends and stories exist about King Arthur than any other king that ever lived. Although some believe that Arthur is just a fantasy hero, he was a very real person and lived somewhere between 470 AD and 530 AD, having been born at Tintagel Castle in Cornwall. It is, however, Cadbury Castle near Glastonbury (said to be the original Camelot) that King Arthur now haunts. On Christmas Eve a phantom figure of King Arthur followed by a troop of armed warriors ride down the hill at South Cadbury and across the fields. They may not always be seen, but the ghostly clatter of horses' hooves and the wail of hunting horns can be heard on a still night.

More than six hundred places in Great Britain claim some association with King Arthur from Wales to Northumberland, and there are numerous burial places that are said to be his grave. At one time the Abbey at Glastonbury had some bones, said to be King Arthur's, along with some locks of Queen Guinevere's hair. Tradition says that King Arthur is not dead, but lies asleep under a hill with his knights waiting for the time when he will be needed to defend Britain. A hillside on the seashore at Llanrhidian, Glamorgan, seems the most likely spot for it is here that the armoured ghost of King Arthur has materialised to startled drivers on the Gower Peninsula road.

KING CHARLES I

If any ghost should appear with its head tucked underneath its arm, you would think that Charles I's would be the most likely candidate! King Charles was beheaded in 1649 and his decapitated body was taken to Windsor to be buried. It is here in the castle grounds that his ghost walks, looking identical to the portraits painted of him by Sir Anthony Van Dyke, and his head is firmly attached!

KING ELLA

In the fifth century AD East Anglia was ruled by a king called Ella. On 21 July 410 his coronation took place on the banks of the River Bure at Horning in Norfolk. Every five years the spectral coronation ceremony is performed again.

KING ETHELBERT

King of East Anglia in the sixth century, Ethelbert was brutally murdered whilst visiting Hereford. Strange things began to happen at the spot where he was buried and a healing spring appeared from his grave. Ethelbert was made a Saint because of this and Hereford Cathedral was built on the site, inside which his ghost has occasionally been spotted.

KING GEORGE II

On 25 October 1760 King George II died at Kensington Palace in London. Born in Germany, King George never felt at home in London and his pale faced ghost appears above the main entrance, still waiting for letters from his native land.

KING GEORGE III

Before his death, King George III went completely mad, and it is his insane ghost that continues to haunt Windsor Castle. The mad King can be heard strumming a harp in a room just below the library (which Queen Elizabeth I haunts), and it has been said by sentries on duty outside the castle that they have heard someone tapping on a window. On looking up they have seen the King's wild eyes looking out at them, presumably hoping that they will come and let him out of his prison.

KING GEORGE IV

It was King George IV who built the magnificent Pavilion in Brighton, which you may have seen. It is not the Pavilion itself which the former Prince Regent haunts, but his ghostly spirit has been seen walking through an underground tunnel that leads from the cellars to the stables.

KING HAROLD II

One of the most memorable dates in history must be 1066, the date of the Battle of Hastings when King Harold is reputed to have been shot in the eye by a Norman arrow. Although the phantom king has been seen at Battle Abbey, his ghost has no sign of eye trouble but instead has a large wound in his right thigh.

KING HENRY VI

During the Wars of the Roses in 1471, King Henry VI was slaughtered in the Tower of London. Since the day of his death he has haunted, not the Tower, but Muncaster Castle in Cumberland where Henry was given refuge by the Pennington family. The Penningtons still own the castle, as they have done for 700 years, and have learnt to live with Henry's ghost. They are protected, however, by a glass bowl called the **'Luck of Muncaster'** with which goes the rhyme:

It shall bless thy bed, it shall bless thy board,
They shall prosper by this token,
In Muncaster Castle good luck shall be
Till this charmed cup be broken.

Nobody ever dare break the Luck of Muncaster!

KING HENRY VIII

Towards the end of his life King Henry VIII was extremely fat and suffered very badly from gout in his legs. He died from an ulcerated leg, caused by a wound in a hunting accident that never healed. Today his groaning ghost can be heard dragging his bad leg around the Deanery at Windsor. His spectre is seldom seen, but frequently heard.

King Henry's ghost has also been heard kicking off his heavy boots in a room in which he slept at the King's Arms, Godalming, Surrey.

KING WILLIAM RUFUS

King William II of England was killed mysteriously in the New Forest and was found with an arrow in his heart. The spot on which he died is marked by a stone known as the Rufus Stone and it is here that the ghost of King William continues to walk. He has also been seen at nearby Castle Malwood where his body was buried. Some say that William was killed during a witchcraft ceremony, but the anniversary of his death (2 August 1100) is when his ghost is most likely to be seen.

Lovelorn Ghosts

LADY ABIGAIL

Four centuries ago the lovely young Lady Abigail of Featherstone Castle fell madly in love with a young man, known as Ridley. Her father disapproved of the match and forced the unhappy Abigail to marry somebody else. As her bridal procession made its way back to the castle, Ridley jumped out of the woods and began to attack Abigail's new husband. In trying to separate the man she loved from the husband she had been made to marry, Abigail was herself killed. Today her ghostly bridal procession can be seen making that fatal journey back to the castle.

ALICE BIRCH

In May 1646, Alice Birch was engaged to a man called Clifford. It was a time of fighting between the Royalists and the Roundheads, and Goodrich Castle, Herefordshire, in which they were hiding came under siege. The lovers decided to escape at night by swimming together across the River Wye. Unfortunately the current dragged them under and the lovers died. Their spectres have been seen many times near the castle.

MARY BLANDY

When Mary Blandy's father forbade her to see the man she loved she poisoned him to death. In 1752 she was hanged for murder, since which time her ghost has haunted the graveyard at Henley-on-Thames where she is buried.

LADY BOSTON

Lady Boston of Boston Manor House in London died mysteriously when her father found her under a giant Cypress tree in the arms of her lover. A shrouded female ghost haunts the manor grounds, disappearing when she reaches the Cypress tree.

MARION DE LA BRUERE

In the twelfth century, the lovesick Marion lowered a rope from her tower at Ludlow Castle, Shropshire, so that her lover, one Arnold de Lys, could climb up. Unfortunately, Arnold was a soldier of an enemy army and after he had climbed up the rope so did more than 100 other enemy soldiers! Ludlow Castle had been captured through one foolish act of love.

Realising what she had done, Marion threw herself from the top of the tower. For eight hundred years her spectre has been seen falling from the tower.

CLARA BURNETT

At the beginning of the eighteenth century Clara Burnett was locked in a room at the Cross Keys Inn, Usk, to keep her away from the man she loved. Clara died of a broken heart and her sobbing spirit still haunts the bedroom in which she died.

FATHER DOMINIQUE

The Crown Inn, Oxford, is haunted by the ghostly apparition of Father Dominique, dressed in a dark cloak. He fought a duel with another man who loved the same girl as he, and lost the fight.

CHARLOTTE DYMOND

If you ever visit Bodmin Moor, Cornwall, look out for a small stone memorial to Charlotte Dymond who met her untimely death in 1844. A young boy called

Matt Weeks was in love with Charlotte, but she did not feel the same for him. One Sunday afternoon she laughed at him and tormented him. He cut her throat. Today her ghost walks the lonely moors as she did on that Sunday afternoon.

ELAINE

The ghost of a young girl known only as Elaine haunts Park House, Haden Hill, Worcestershire. In Tudor times Elaine fell in love with a Monk from nearby Manor Abbey. They met secretly in the cellar of Park House to plan their wedding, but accidentally got locked in and starved to death.

SARAH FLETCHER

In June 1799 young Sarah Fletcher hanged herself from the rail of her four-poster bed at Clifton Hampden in Oxford, when she discovered that the man she loved planned to marry someone else. Her auburn-haired spectre tearfully haunts the bedroom.

KITTY GARTHWAITE

On Whit Sunday 1787, Kitty Garthwaite threw herself into the river Dove in North Yorkshire when her boyfriend, Willie Dixon, deserted her. Four days later Willie jumped in to the river at the same spot. For many years Kitty's ghost appeared by the riverside and lured men to their deaths. Eventually her ghost was exorcised.

LADY ELIZABETH GRAY

Having fallen in love with a coachman, Lady Elizabeth eloped from The George Inn, Silsoe, Bedfordshire, at midnight in his coach. In their haste to get away the coach crashed into a lake, which Lady Elizabeth has haunted ever since.

LADY CONSTANCE HALL

In the thirteenth century Sir Thomas Hall was gored to death by a wild stag. His wife, Lady Constance, was so heartbroken that she threw herself from a tower of their home, Hall Place, Bexley. Her ghost re-enacts her death fall and her ghostly moans still echo around the building.

LADY JANE

At a place called Hope, Clwyd in Wales, two men fought a duel because they both loved the beautiful Lady Jane. Sadly, the man that Lady Jane loved herself was killed in the duel, the other survived. Not wishing to marry him she jumped into a well and died. She now haunts the well.

LUCETTE

In the eighteenth century Lucette, a young French girl, came over from France to be nursemaid to some children at Dunkenhalgh Park House, Clayton Le Moors, in Lancashire. She fell in love with the soldier son of the family, who soon afterwards went away to war. After six months had passed, Lucette felt that she could no longer wait for his return and she threw herself into the river Hyndburn. Today her ghost can be seen by a small stone bridge on the river.

MARGARET REAY

Margaret Reay's portrait hangs in Admiralty House, London, which she haunts. On 7 April 1779 she was shot dead by a jealous lover whilst leaving the theatre at Covent Garden, but it is her former home which houses her spectre.

DONNA OVIEDO

Known as the **'Green Lady of Louth'**, Donna fell in love with Sir John Bolles in Cadiz, 1596. John returned to England without her. Donna plunged a dagger into her heart. Her ghost followed him to England and haunted his home of Thorpe Hall, Lincolnshire, until his death, and has continued to haunt it ever since.

JULIET TOUSLEY

In 1050 a beautiful young nineteen-year-old girl called Juliet, fell in love with a woodcutter named Tom Zoul. When it became apparent that Tom did not share the same feelings, Juliet hanged herself from a willow tree, and was buried beneath it. The Ferry Boat Inn at Holywell, Huntingdonshire, now covers the spot and it is there on the anniversary of her death, 17 March, that Juliet's ghost appears.

Monster Madness

How do monsters count to twenty-eight?

On their fingers.

Where do monsters study?

At ghoullege.

What do vampires cross the sea in?

Blood vessels.

Why did the boy monster push his father into the deep freeze?

Because he wanted iced pop.

Why did the boy monster push his father's finger into an electric socket?

Because he wanted fizzy pop.

What did the mother monster say to her son?

'Don't sit in that chair, it's for Rigor Mortis to set in.'

Where does Dracula stay when he visits New York?

The Vampire State Building.

What is the ghost's favourite pub?

The horse and gloom.

What goes ha-ha-ha plonk?

A monster laughing its head off.

What did the monster eat after the dentist took all his teeth out?

The dentist.

Who said 'Shiver me timbers!' on the phantom ship?

The skeleton crew.

What trees do ghouls prefer?

Ceme-trees.

What is a monster's favourite dessert?

Leeches and scream.

What do you call a beautiful, polite monster?

A failure.

Why did Frankenstein's monster give up boxing?

He didn't want to spoil his looks.

'Mummy, mummy, what's a werewolf?'

'Be quiet, and comb your face.'

'Mummy, mummy, what's a vampire?'

'Shut up and drink your soup before it clots.'

'Mummy, mummy, daddy's just gone out.'

'Well put some more paraffin on him then.'

Who puts the ghosts' point of view at a press conference?

The spooksman.

What is a gargoyle?

Something you take when you have a sore throat.

Why did the monster go to the wedding?

So he could toast the guests.

Why do skeleton's like parties?

Because they have a rattling good time.

Which ices do ghosts prefer?

I-screams for help.

If you were surrounded by a headless ghost, a vampire, a werewolf, and a phantom white lady, what would you do?

Cross your fingers and hope that it's a fancy dress party.

A murderer was sitting in the electric chair waiting to be executed. 'Have you any last request?' asked the chaplain.

'Yes,' said the murderer, 'will you hold my hand?'

Where do you find vampire's nails?

On the end of vampire's fingers.

Why was the Egyptian girl worried?

Because her daddy was a mummy.

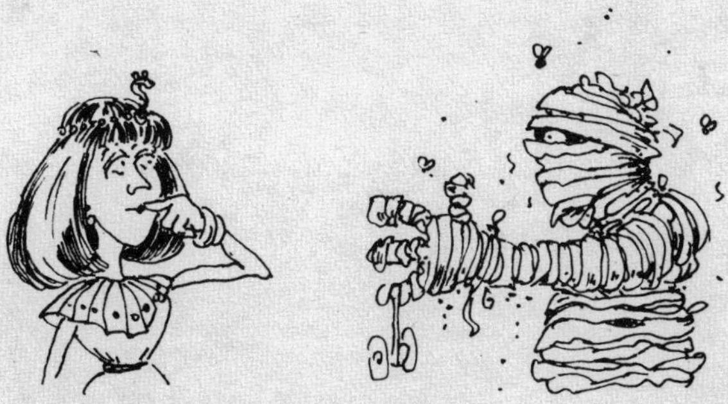

Name That Ghost

. . . Ghostly definitions.

This ghostly guide will help you understand the world of the supernatural.

AMULET

A lucky charm that is worn to ward off evil spirits. It can be anything from a jewel to a rabbit's foot.

APPARITION

A supernatural being that can be human or animal. Ghosts are apparitions, but apparitions are not always ghosts, for occasionally the vision of someone still living can appear. Usually this will happen when the person is in danger or needs help.

ASTRAL BODY

This is our spirit body which leaves our real body when we die. Sometimes our astral body will leave our own while we are asleep. We remember the experience next day as dreams.

APPORTATION

This is when a material object appears from nowhere. Sometimes solid objects move mysteriously from one room to another, but nobody quite knows how.

BANSHEE

A faceless ghost that makes a loud mournful wail on the eve of someone's death. They are more common in Scotland and Ireland.

BLACK MAGIC

This is evil magic performed by witches and devil worshippers who want to bring only harm to others.

CLAIRVOYANT

The word means **'clear seer'**, and means someone who has extraordinary powers and can see pictures of events that will happen. Sometimes clairvoyants can see and speak to the spirits of the dead.

CORPSE LIGHTS

Sometimes the spirit of someone recently buried can be seen hovering over their grave as a very faint light.

DOPPELGANGER

The name given to the apparition of a living person. If a person sees his or her own doppelganger it means that they will soon die.

DRYAD

A spirit that lives in a tree or bush (woods and forests are full of them) and dies as soon as the plant dies.

ECTOPLASM

During a seance (a meeting of people trying to communicate with the dead) ectoplasm will come from the mouth of the medium. It is like a white mist that forms itself into the shape of a human face or even a whole person.

EXORCISM

A ceremony performed by a priest to drive out an evil spirit.

EXTRA-SENSORY PERCEPTION

Sometimes we say that people are psychic or have **ESP**, which means that they get a feeling that something is going to happen before it actually does.

FETCH

The double or **'doppelganger'** of a person soon to die.

FOLKLORE

Legends and stories about ghosts and superstitions that have existed for centuries and are believed by many even today.

GALLOWS GHOST

The spectre of someone who was hanged, usually at a crossroads. They remain where their execution took place.

GHOUL

An evil spirit that haunts graveyards and feeds on dead bodies.

GRAVEYARD GUARDIAN

The ghost of the very first person buried in a graveyard is said to haunt it and keep evil spirits away.

HAUNTING

This is the term used when the same ghost visits the same place over and over again.

HALLOWE'EN

31 October, the night when witches and warlocks are said to abound. Thousands of years ago it was believed that on this night the gates to the Underworld were opened to let the spirits of the dead in, and evil spirits out.

HORSESHOE

A popular amulet or good luck charm. It should be nailed to your house with the open end pointing upwards to keep the good luck in.

INTUITION

A sixth-sense that many animals have and a few people, when you get a strong feeling that you know whether somebody is good or very bad.

JINX

Something that brings bad luck. The opposite to an amulet.

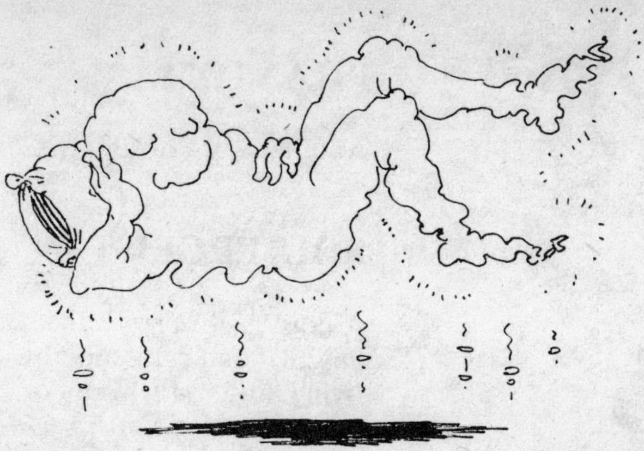

LEVITATION

When someone, or something, has the power to raise itself off the ground and hang suspended in mid-air on its own.

MEDIUM

Someone who has the power to communicate with the spirits of the dead.

OCCULT

A general term used to cover anything to do with magic or the supernatural.

PARANORMAL

Another word meaning '**Supernatural**', or something that we cannot really explain.

PHANTOM

Another word meaning **'Ghost'**.

POLTERGEIST

A noisy, active spirit that causes mischief and can send objects flying around the room or crashing to the floor.

PREMONITION

A vision of something awful that is going to happen.

PSYCHOKINESIS

Mind over matter. The power to make material objects move or alter their shape without touching them, but by just willing them to do so.

REVENANT

A ghost that was wronged during life and returns to carry out revenge.

SEANCE

A meeting in which a number of people gather together to try to communicate with the dead.

SPECTRE

An apparition of somebody dead.

SUPERSTITION

A strange belief concerning good or bad luck. For example, some people think it is unlucky to walk under a ladder, to break a mirror or spill salt. They are all superstitions.

TELEPATHY

The power to transmit thoughts. There are occasions when you know what a person is thinking, or what they are going to say before they actually say it. Twins are sometimes telepathic and are able to read each other's thoughts.

VAMPIRE

A dead body that comes to life again. It comes out of its coffin at night and sucks blood to keep alive. It must return to its coffin before dawn.

WARLOCK

A male witch.

WRAITH

An apparition or doppelganger that means a death will occur.

WEREWOLF

A creature that is man by day and turns into a wolf at night.

ZOMBIE

The living dead. Dead bodies returned to life by evil sorcerers, they are dumb and have a blank eerie look on their faces.

Once Upon A Time . . . .

. . . . Ghostly tall stories

A very brave man once agreed to spend the night in a house that was said to be haunted. In the middle of the night he was woken from his sleep by a weird rapping noise. It seemed to be coming from somewhere above him, so he decided to investigate.

He put on his dressing gown and ventured out on to the landing. The rapping noise continued and seemed to be coming from the attic. The man tip-toed up the rickety steps to the attic, which was in pitch blackness. The rapping noise went on. Lighting a candle the man made his way through the cobwebs and gloom of the attic to a small box on a table, from where the rapping noise seemed to be coming. Very very slowly he approached the box and gently lifted the lid, trembling as he peered inside to find. . . . **a piece of wrapping paper!**

* * *

Three little boys, Michael, Adrian and Alexander, were playing cricket one day in a field on the edge of a large wood. Adrian hit the ball with all his might and it shot straight past his two friends and into the wood. Alexander was just about to go in and retrieve the ball when Michael said: 'Be very careful, there's a ghost in there with one black eye and it might get you.'

'You can't frighten me!' said Alexander, running into the wood. No sooner had he started looking around for the ball than an eerie voice began to howl:

'I am the ghost with one black eye, and if you don't leave the wood I shall haunt you forever.'

Alexander turned pale and ran out of the wood as fast as his legs would carry him.

'There . . . there's . . . there's a ghost in there!' he stuttered.

'Oh, don't be such a baby!' said Adrian, and he ran into the wood to look for the ball. No sooner had he started looking around than the eerie voice howled:

'I am the ghost with one black eye, and if you don't leave the wood I shall haunt you forever.'

Adrian turned on his heels and ran out of the wood as fast as he could.

'You two really are cowards!' said Michael, and he strode boldly into the wood. No sooner had he started looking for the ball, than the eerie voice howled again:

'I am the ghost with one black eye and if you don't leave the wood I shall haunt you forever.'

'And if you don't let me find the ball,' yelled Michael, 'You'll be the ghost with **two** black eyes!'

* * *

A rabbit was walking down a road one day, when suddenly he felt very hungry. Being tired of lettuce and carrots he decided to visit a little inn and see what food they had to offer. He walked straight in and asked the landlord if there was anything to eat.

'Yes,' said the landlord, 'today we have toasties on

the menu. You can have a ham toastie, a mushroom toastie or a cheese toastie.'

'Oh, I'll have a cheese toastie, please,' said the rabbit, 'and a pint of shandy.'

The rabbit took his toastie and sat in the corner with his shandy and soon polished them both off hungrily. Within five minutes he was back at the bar.

'I'll have a mushroom toastie and another shandy,' said the rabbit.

The landlord looked surprised, but gave the rabbit his order and he returned to his table.

Ten minutes later the rabbit returned to the bar.

'I'll have a ham toastie, landlord, and another pint of shandy.'

The landlord gave the rabbit the toastie and the drink and watched him return to his corner seat and polish them off. No sooner had the rabbit had his last mouthful of toastie than he fell off his stool flat on the floor. Thinking the rabbit must be drunk the landlord rushed over to throw him out, but discovered that the rabbit was dead! Not knowing what to do, he took the rabbit to his garden at the back of the inn and buried him.

That evening the bar was full of people, when suddenly to everyone's horror the ghost of the rabbit walked through the wall and up to the bar. Everybody fled in terror, but the landlord was trapped behind the bar.

'Was there something the matter with your drink?' stuttered the landlord.

'No,' replied the rabbit ghost, 'I died from **mixin' matoasties**.'

* * *

One dark winter's evening Tanya arrived home from school early to find the house totally empty. She took off her coat and drew the curtains as it was dark and cold outside. Suddenly a loud noise made her nearly jump out of her skin — it was the telephone. On lifting the receiver Tanya heard a ghoulish voice say:

'My name is Bleeding-Finger and I'm coming to get you in ten minutes.'

She slammed the receiver down in horror. The next thing she heard were loud slow footsteps coming up the path outside and a voice saying:

'My name is Bleeding-Finger and I'm coming to get you in five minutes!'

Tanya screamed and ran upstairs as fast as her legs would go. She ran into her bedroom, slammed the door and lay on her bed trembling.

Next she heard the breaking of glass as something smashed its way through the front door, and the heavy thud of footsteps made their way up the stairs.

'My name is Bleeding-Finger and I'm coming to get you!' As Tanya squeezed herself under her bed she saw her bedroom door being pushed open very very slowly, and first a foot came round the door, then a leg, then some vast horrible creature. A creature uglier than she had ever seen in her life, covered in hair, and with one finger pouring with blood.

'My name is Bleeding-Finger and I've come to get you!' it moaned.

'Why? What do you want with me?' trembled Tanya.

'Could you put a bandage on my finger, please?'

Phantom Stagecoach

Ghosts appear in many shapes and forms, and it's not only buildings that are haunted, but many roads too. Almost every part of the country seems to have a road down which a phantom stagecoach drives, usually complete with headless driver and sometimes a headless occupant too, as you will discover if you read the story of Anne Boleyn later in this book.

Here are the stories of some more phantom vehicles. . . .

THE BLACK GREVE CHARIOT

At midnight on Christmas Eve if you are ever at Black Greve Farm near Birmingham you will hear the deathly screams coming from a spectral Roman chariot that crashed in 47 AD, killing its occupants. The grisly crash is repeated every year.

PHANTOM BUS

A more modern **'stagecoach'**, a number 7 red London bus used to be seen driving through Kensington in London. Until the road at the junction of St. Mark's Road and Cambridge Gardens was straightened, car drivers would turn the corner to encounter a driverless and passengerless bus careering towards them. They crashed swerving to avoid the bus, which promptly vanished. Over one hundred accidents happened in a short space of time because of the phantom bus.

LADY CAREW'S COACH

On 31 May 1741, Lady Montefiore Carew was forced by her mother to marry Sir Godfrey Haslitt, a man whom she hated. On the way back from the marriage ceremony in Norwich Cathedral, the bridal coach crashed into Potter Heigham Bridge at the village of Bastwick, Norfolk. Every year on the 31 May a phantom stagecoach drives through the village, with skeletons inside, and crashes into the bridge.

DOGGETT'S CORPSE

In Dorset at the village of Tarrant Gunville is a house called Eastbury, once a magnificent palace of a house. It was here that William Doggett worked as a steward and began to steal from his master. When he was discovered he took a gun and blew out his brains. Now on the anniversary of his death a coach drawn by a headless coachman drives up to the house, rattling over the cattle grid on its way, and here it picks up the ghostly corpse of William Doggett. In 1845 William Doggett's coffin was opened. His corpse was red-cheeked and showed no sign of decay, causing many to believe that Doggett was a vampire and comes alive at night.

LADY HOWARD'S COACH

In the seventeenth century, Lady Howard of Fitzford House, Tavistock in Devon was married four times. She murdered each of her four husbands. Since her death her spectre has been seen driving a coach that seems to be made of bones and is pulled by headless horses. She drives between Okehampton Castle and her former home. Tradition says that she is collecting the souls of the dead and bringing them to Okehampton.

SNAKE PASS COACH

Snake Pass in Derbyshire got its name because its bendy roads wind like a snake. It is here that drivers have suddenly encountered a phantom horse and cart with a driver wearing a top hat. As soon as they have tried to overtake the cart, it has vanished into thin air.

PHANTOM FUNERAL PROCESSIONS

There are a number of phantom funeral processions that take place. On dark December evenings at the town of Bedworth in the Midlands a horse-drawn hearse followed by a procession of mourners in horse drawn carriages make their way down Wootton Street and vanish. It appears to be a ghost from the Edwardian era that has continued through the decades.

The most famous funeral procession is that of Sir Piers Legh who died at the Battle of Agincourt in

1415. His body was brought home to Lyme Park in Cheshire where his phantom funeral is now seen. His coffin is pulled in a coach and is followed by a woman in white, said to be Blanche, the woman he loved, who died of a broken heart on hearing of his death.

MARY TUDOR

Queen of England from 1553 to 1558, she was known as 'Bloody Mary' — but her ghost which appears in the tapestry room of Sawston Hall, Cambridge, is surprisingly un-bloody. Probably because it was in this house that her life was saved when the owners helped her escape, disguised as a milkmaid. Her smiling ghost is not only seen, but can be heard playing the harpsichord.

Queenly Ghosts

QUEEN BOADICEA

On the Embankment in London close to the Houses of Parliament is a statue of Queen Boadicea in her chariot. In the small village of Cammeringham, near Lincoln, this is exactly how the ghost of Queen Boadicea is said to appear as she is seen riding through the mists standing on her chariot. This wraith is known popularly as **'The Cammeringham Light'** and appears on a stretch of Roman road along which Boadicea would most certainly have ridden.

QUEEN ANNE BOLEYN

The popular image we have of ghosts is that of someone with their head tucked underneath their arm, and Anne Boleyn who lost her head on 19 May 1536 certainly fits the bill for her headless ghost can be seen at a number of haunts. On the anniversary of her death she arrives at Blickling Hall in Norfolk in a phantom black coach, pulled by headless horses and driven by a headless coachman; she wears a white dress and carries her decapitated head, resting it in her lap. She pulls up at the house, leaves the coach and glides through the corridors of Blickling, where she spent her happy childhood. Anne's ghost can also be seen at the White Tower, Tower Green and St. Peter-Ad-Vincula at the Tower of London where her remains now lie, and she has been sighted at Hampton Court, Windsor Castle, Hever Castle, Rochford Hall, and Bollin Hall. A story says that one night at the Tower of London two sentries saw a light in the chapel of St. Peter-Ad-Vincula one night, and on looking in through the window they saw a phantom procession of people in Tudor dress led by Anne Boleyn. As they watched, the light began to fade and the people vanished.

QUEEN CATHERINE OF ARAGON

First wife of Henry VIII, Catherine was banished to Buckden Palace in Huntingdonshire on Henry's marriage to Anne Boleyn. So distressed was she that she died a year later in 1536 and has continued to haunt a small room next to the chapel.

QUEEN ELIZABETH I

The ghostly vision of 'Good Queen Bess' can still be seen walking through the library in the State Apartments of Windsor Castle. People reading in the library have heard footsteps and looking up have seen the Queen gliding towards them. A phantom coach has also been seen driving the ghostly spectre from Greenwich to her hunting lodge in Epping forest. Richmond Palace, the place of her death is where her ghost is most often seen. Dying in 1603 with the immortal words 'All my possessions for a moment in time', her spectre has since been seen walking through the apartments, and on the anniversary of her death her wraith appears at the gatehouse from where her ring was thrown to a horserider to take to King James IV of Scotland to inform him that he was now King of England too.

QUEEN CATHERINE HOWARD

Fifth wife of Henry VIII, like Anne Boleyn she too lost her head on Tower Green. She was executed on 13 February 1542. Whilst being held prisoner at Hampton Court she managed to escape from her guards and ran down the corridors to the chapel where Henry VIII was praying, hoping to beg for mercy. She beat the door with her fists until the guards dragged her off screaming. Her screams have echoed down the centuries, and her desperate ghost has been seen running through what is now known as the Haunted Gallery.

QUEEN ISABELLA

Queen Isabella was the wife of Edward II. She haunts Castle Rising in Norfolk and can be seen walking along the castle walls. Strangely enough she is laughing, and her maniacal laughter rings out through the night. She is buried in Greyfriars Churchyard in London, where she can be seen walking, apparently carrying the heart of her murdered husband.

MARY, QUEEN OF SCOTS

One of the saddest queens, Mary spent many years being imprisoned in castles all over England before finally being beheaded at Fotheringhay Castle in 1587. Her ghost haunts many of the places in which she was imprisoned. At Palace House, Beaulieu, Hampshire, her ghostly footsteps can be heard running down a staircase as she re-enacts her escape. She also haunts Nappa Hall, Wensleydale; The Haycock, Wansford; Bolton Castle, and Southwick House which was once connected to Fotheringhay Castle by a secret tunnel. When the castle was destroyed, much of the timber and a staircase used by Mary were used to decorate the Talbot Inn at Oundle. With the timbers came the ghost of Mary, Queen of Scots, and she now continues to haunt this Northamptonshire inn.

QUEEN JANE SEYMOUR

Third wife of Henry VIII, Jane died in 1537 after only one year of marriage whilst giving birth to Henry's only son, Edward. The ghost of Jane, dressed all in white, has been seen carrying a lighted candle wandering through the Queen's apartments at Hampton Court. She is also said to haunt Marwell Hall in Hampshire, her former home.

R.I.P. Graveyard Tales

One night on the edge of a remote country village a storm was raging. The thunder roared, lightning flashed, and the rain lashed down in torrents. A man on his way home suddenly had the misfortune to get a flat tyre on his car. He decided to abandon the car for the night and walk home to his cottage on the other side of the village. Because the weather was so bad, he decided to take a short cut through the graveyard. It was very spooky with lightning flashing on the gravestones, so he turned up his collar and hurried on. Suddenly, however, his attention was caught by a loud tap-tapping sound that appeared to be coming from behind one of the gravestones. Frightened though he was, his curiosity got the better of him and he peeped behind the gravestone. There was a strange looking man draped in a white sheet. The trembling motorist looked closer at the creature lit up by the lightning flashes — in his hands were a hammer and chisel.

'What are you doing?' asked the motorist.

'I'm just correcting the headstone,' said the creature, 'They've spelt my name wrong. . . .'

* * *

Two little boys were returning home one evening at dusk after having collected a great big bag full of conkers. They decided that they ought to share the conkers out evenly between them, as they had both worked so hard collecting them, so they went into the graveyard to count them out. As they went in the gate one of the boys dropped the bag and two conkers rolled just outside the gate.

'Don't worry about those, we'll collect them later,' said the boy.

They then sat behind a tombstone and started to count out the conkers. While they were counting them, a little girl happened to be walking through the graveyard and as she passed the tombstone she heard a voice say,

'One for you, and one for me. One for you, and one for me. . . .'

Hardly daring to breathe, she ran towards the gate where she saw her friend standing.

'What's the matter?' asked her friend.

'Oh, Miriam, it's awful! There are two ghosts in the graveyard and they're sharing out dead bodies.' As she pointed towards the tombstone they heard a voice say,

'One for you, and one for me. And we mustn't forget those two down by the gate!'

* * *

A village doctor was walking through the churchyard one evening when he saw a gravedigger drinking a bottle of beer.

'How dare you drink alcohol in the churchyard!' shouted the doctor, 'I shall complain to the vicar about this.'

'I wouldn't do that if I was you,' said the gravedigger, 'considering all the blunders I cover up for you!'

* * *

A doctor once lived next door to a hypochondriac who was the plague of his life for every night the man would knock on the doctor's bedroom wall and shout:

'Have you got anything for an upset stomach?' or

'Have you got anything for a splitting headache?' Suddenly one day the man died unexpectedly, which came as quite a relief to the doctor. At last he thought he would get some peace. Unfortunately, within two days the doctor had died himself and was buried in the grave next to the hypochondriac. On his first night there came a tapping on the side of the doctor's coffin and a voice said:

'Have you got anything for worms?'

Tell this joke to your friends in a quiet, soft voice until you get to the very last line and then **SHOUT!** They will jump out of their skins!

Two very evil and wicked men decided to go one night to the graveyard and dig up the body of a woman buried there so that they could steal a valuable diamond ring that was on her finger. They crept into the cemetery at the stroke of midnight, dug up the coffin and tried to remove the ring from the corpse. It wouldn't come off. Desperate to get the ring they chopped off the finger, and with the ring safely in their possession they ran from the grave. Suddenly a terrible storm started brewing, and not wishing to spend the night in the cold and wet they knocked on the door of a remote farm house. An ugly old hag opened the door and they asked if they could have a bed for the night. She let them in and took them into a dark kitchen, lit by one small lamp.

'Would you like some supper?' asked the old hag.

'Yes, please,' said the men, quite hungry after their digging.

As the woman started to get some food they noticed that on one hand she had a finger missing. They looked at each other in terror.

'What happened to your finger?' asked one of the graverobbers nervously.

The old hag turned and stared at the men, her eyes like fire in the glow of the lamplight as she said:

'YOU'VE GOT IT!'

Spooky Places

LADY ANNE'S GRAVE, Hertfordshire.

Lady Anne Grimston's grave at Tewin is a strange place to visit. Lady Anne did not believe in God, and when she died in November 1716, she said that if there was any truth in the word of God seven trees would grow from her grave. If you visit her grave in the churchyard you will see that seven trees have forced their way through her tomb.

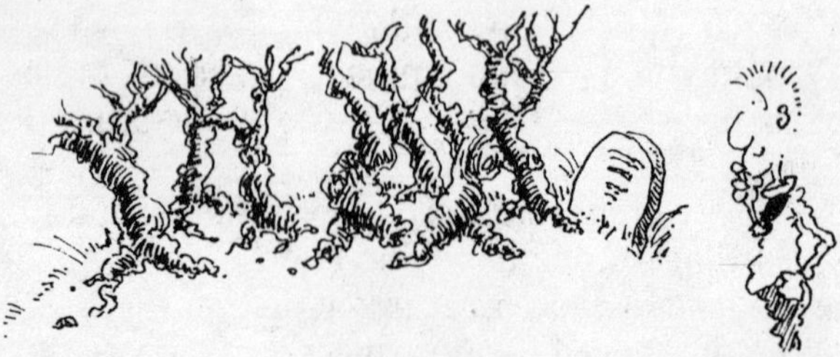

BETTY'S GRAVE, Gloucestershire.

Near Cirencester at the point of a cross roads is an uncanny place known as Betty's Grave. Betty was a witch called Elizabeth Bastre who was buried in 1786, after being hanged for witchcraft. Avoid the spot just in case she decides to cast a spell on you!

BURFORD, Oxfordshire.

This village is a particularly spooky place, for not only are there horrific screams heard ringing out through the graveyard at night, bells tolled by unseen hands, the chants of ghostly monks, but also a terrifying ghostly black cloud that can completely surround you. Nasty!

CLASSENWELL, Devon.

This spooky place should be avoided at all costs, especially at night, for it is here that a ghostly voice cries out the name of the next person who is going to die. That's something we would rather not know.

DOZMARY POOL, Cornwall.

This mysterious pool in the middle of Bodmin Moor has a long history, and is said to be the lake in which King Arthur's sword **Excalibur** was thrown by Sir Bedivere. The atmosphere at this pool sends a chill through the blood of anyone who visits it, and is said to be haunted by the spectre of Lord Robartes, whose hapless spirit has to empty Dozmary Pool for eternity with a limpet shell.

HEDDON OAK TREE, Somerset.

At the strange sounding village of Stogumber is a large oak tree, known as the Heddon Oak. It was from the bough of this tree that centuries ago some of the Duke of Monmouth's soldiers were hanged. If you stand under this tree you feel as if you are being strangled.

THE LYCH WAY, Dartmoor.

If you go to Devil's Tor on Dartmoor you will find a narrow track going in a south-westerly direction to Lydford Churchyard. It was along this track that the bodies of the dead were taken to be buried, and in winter were sometimes left on the track in the snow because the weather was too bad to continue. The ghosts of these long dead people still walk the Lych Way.

RIVER PARRETT, Somerset.

Never walk along the banks of the River Parrett at Combwich, for a ghost that lurks beneath the waters is said to claim the life of one child, one woman and one man every year.

MONEY LANE, Cambridgeshire.

Money Lane at Horseheath is said to have buried treasure, but is haunted by the person who buried it. A ghostly voice says '*Pick up your spade and follow me*,' but nobody dares. They might be going to dig a grave. . . . their own!

SACKMORE LANE, Wiltshire.

In 1870 a pit full of human bones was discovered near Sackmore Lane at Marnhull. This was probably a grave that was used during the time of the Great Plague. Along this lane two ghosts make their way towards the pit carrying a coffin.

TRAP'S HILL, Essex.

On Trap's Hill, near Loughton, the wraith of highwayman Dick Turpin can be seen dragging a woman behind him. He is trying to discover where her jewelry is hidden. Beware that he doesn't try and haunt you.

SHARD GATE, Dorset.

At Chettle Down in Dorset a fight took place when a gamekeeper discovered a poacher. In the battle the poacher escaped after having his hand chopped off. The man eventually died and was buried in London, although his hand remained in the Dorset churchyard. At Shard Gate the ghostly hand is often seen trying to find its lost body.

WICKFORD ROUNDABOUT, Essex.

A few years ago a girl was killed in a motorcycle accident at this roundabout. Today she appears, apparently hitchhiking. If any car stops to give her a lift, she disappears.

Things That Go Bump In The Night

Most ghosts are silent. They make no noise as they silently glide through the house. Occasionally, however, something goes bump in the night. This is no ordinary ghost, but something that we call a **POLTERGEIST**.

'*Geist*' is the German word for *ghost*, and '*Polter*' means *noise*, so a *Poltergeist* is a *ghost that makes a noise*. They are very mischievous spirits and not only do they make bangs and crashes in the night to let you know that they are there, but they can send objects flying around the room, pull bedclothes off the bed, cause light bulbs to swing, start fires, and even hide things so that they cannot be found.

One of the most famous poltergeists appeared in 1662 at the home of a judge called John Mompesson. He had arrested a drummer called William Drury for being a tramp, and had his drum taken away from him. The drum was kept at the magistrate's house and in the middle of the night it started to play on its own. Judge Mompesson smashed the drum and immediately things began flying around the room. For exactly one year there were strange noises every night to disturb the judge, then suddenly for no reason they stopped.

* * *

Even in recent years modern houses have been plagued with poltergeist activity, as at the West London home of Mr. and Mrs. Francis Tryon. On the evening of August 11th 1983 Mrs. Tryon was in the house with her thirteen year old daughter Katie, when they heard the sound of heavy footsteps upstairs. On investigation they found the rooms empty, but as they watched the wardrobe door flew open and a chair was pushed across the room. Then for no reason the mirror shattered. For the next month the Tryon family were subjected to loud banging noises in the middle of the night, bedclothes were pulled over their heads in the middle of the night and tried to suffocate them, things moved mysteriously from room to room without being seen, and strange muttering sounds could be heard when someone was alone in the house.

An investigator into psychic matters was called into the house and was able to communicate with the spirit. He discovered that it was the ghost of a woman called Emily Dobson who had died in the upstairs bedroom. She had come back to find her children, who had since moved away. Once she realised that her children no longer lived there the activities stopped. Hopefully the restless spirit will never return.

* * *

One of the most disturbing poltergeists became active at Calvados Castle in October 1875. On the 13th of October the owner of the house sat writing his diary late at night, when he heard someone knocking. Before he could discover where the sound was coming from a candlestick flew across the room and a heavy armchair fell over on its back. As the days progressed the poltergeist activity got worse. There were mysterious bangings, loud shrieks and moans, windows were smashed, books flew off the shelves and were torn in mid air, doors slammed and mysteriously locked themselves.

Eventually the activities became so bad that a priest was called in to exorcise the wicked spirit. A religious medallion was used to frighten off the spirit. Without warning the medallion was thrown through the air, and the poltergeist disappeared forever.

Ugh.

To haunt your own family and friends, here are some horrifying sound effects that you can make. Why not write your own ghost story and then read it aloud, using the following sounds to make it seem really spooky!

RATTLING BONES

To create the sound of a ghostly skeleton, simply take four or five pencils or crayons. Tie each pencil on to a piece of string about 15 cm long. Hold the strings in one hand and rattle the pencils together. They will sound like hollow bones.

HOWLING WIND

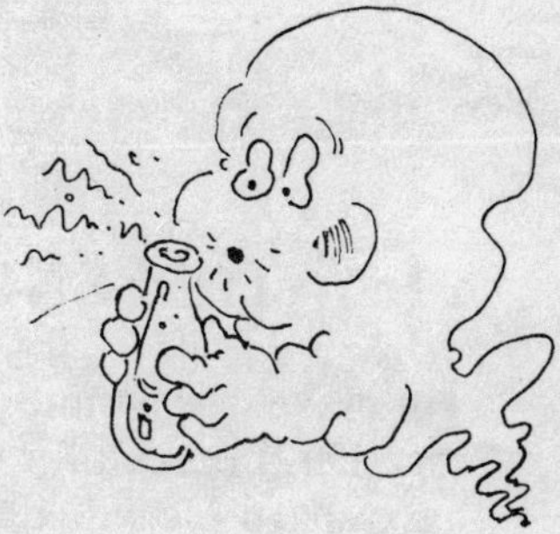

Take an empty milk bottle and blow gently over the rim. You will find that it makes an eerie noise like the moaning wind. By putting some water in the bottle you can change the sound. Different amounts of water will create a new sound.

CLANKING CHAINS

All you need is a length of chain. The kind of thick chain that you lock up a bicycle with is ideal. Drag it along the ground to make a horrible clanking sound.

WEREWOLF

Werewolves make a horrible howling sound like a wolf baying to the moon. You can make this sound yourself by howling really loudly, but if you have a pet dog you can get them to help you! The next time your dog howls get a tape recorder and record the sound he makes. When you play it back, turn the volume up really loud for a blood-curdling noise.

PHANTOM KNIGHT

To make the sound of clanking armour, gather together three or four tin cans. **NEVER** use cans that have sharp jagged edges, but pick empty cocoa tins that have a lid. Get an adult to put a hole for you in each tin and lid, so that you can thread them all on to a length of string. Put on a can then knot the string. Thread on a lid and knot the string again. Continue until all your cans and lids have been knotted on securely. Now let them all clank together to create the clanking of a phantom knight's armour. If you can do this in a room that has an echo it will sound even better!

GLIDING GHOST

A handful of dried peas or lentils and an old shoe box can be used to make a particularly spine chilling sound, especially if you do it in the middle of the night when all is quiet. Simply let the peas slide slowly from one end of the box to the other, and back again. It will sound like the rustling of an Elizabethan lady's dress.

SCREEEEEECH!

If you have an old violin or stringed instrument you can make a terrifying screech. Lie the violin on a table. Tie one end of a piece of string to a door handle, and the other end to a weight. Hang the string over the violin strings and when someone opens the door the string will move over the violin. Screeeeeeeeech!

THUNDER CLAPS

From a hardware shop, or perhaps even from your garage or garden shed, you might be able to get a piece of hardboard. Any kind of board will do, as long as it is bendy. If you grip the board with one hand on each side and rattle it, it will sound like the rumbling of thunder. You can do the same thing with the lid of an old biscuit tin, too.

When making ghostly sound effects, why not tape record them all to make your own horror sound track. If you use your bathroom as a recording studio your recordings will take on an even more spooky quality.

Verse — and Worse

Here are the graves of three poor sinners.
They died after eating our school dinners.

There were three ghostesses
Sitting on postesses
Eating buttered toastesses
And greasing their fistesses
Right up to their wristesses
Weren't they beastesses
To make such feastesses.

The bomb he set went off too soon,
And here his story ceases.
The bits they found are buried here —
So thus he Rests In Pieces.

Here lies a man who met his fate
Because he put on too much weight;
To over eating he was prone
But now he's gained his final STONE.

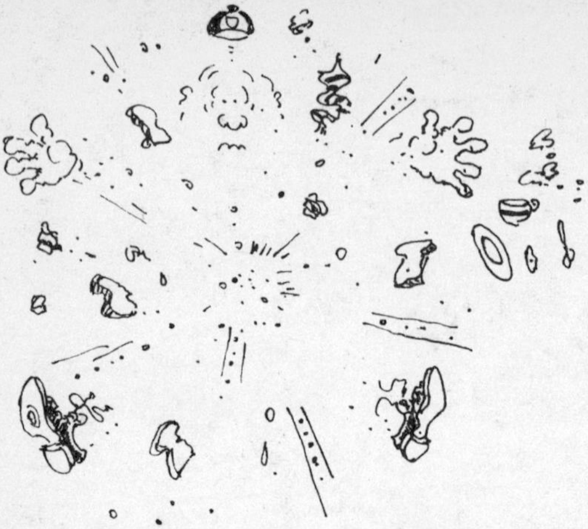

The Boy Stood In the Supper Room

The boy stood in the supper room
Whence all but he had fled;
He'd eaten seven pots of jam
And he was gorged with bread.

'Oh, one more crust before I bust!'
He cried in accents wild;
He licked the plates, he sucked the spoons —
He was a vulgar child.

There came a burst of thunder-sound —
The boy — oh! where was he?
Ask of the maid who mopped him up,
The bread crumbs and the tea!

ANON.

A silly young fellow named Hyde
In a funeral procession was spied;
When asked, 'Who is dead?'
He giggled and said:
'I don't know; I just came for the ride.'

Little Willie from his mirror
Sucked the mercury all off,
Thinking, in his childish error,
It would cure his whooping cough.

At the funeral Willie's mother
Smartly said to Mrs. Brown:
'Twas a chilly day for Willie
When the mercury went down.'

This is the grave of Pat O'Flynn,
Who carefully removed the pin,
But sent himself straight up to Heaven
By counting ten instead of seven.

Beside him lies his only son,
Who robbed a bank to help his Mum.
He sawed the wrong end off his gun,
And blew himself to Kingdom come.

There was an old man who averred
He had learned how to fly like a bird.
Cheered by thousands of people
He leapt from a steeple —
His tomb states the date it occurred.

A novice was driving a car,
When, down Porlock, his son said 'Papa,
If you drive at this rate
We are bound to be late —
Drive faster!' — He did, and they are!

Lady Jane Grey
Had little to say.
What **could** *she have said*
After losing her head?

Walter Raleigh and other Famous Ghosts

FRED ARCHER

Newmarket racecourse is haunted by the ghost of the famous Victorian jockey, Fred Archer. During his short lifetime he rode over 2,000 winners, and although he died in 1886 at the age of twenty-nine he still continues to ride his favourite grey horse around the course one hundred years later, causing a number of horses to shy and fall during a race.

THOMAS À BECKET

Although brutally murdered in Canterbury Cathedral in 1170 after quarrelling with Henry II (and you can still see the spot on which this happened if you visit the cathedral today) strangely enough his ghost haunts the ruined castle at Hastings where he was once Dean. His ghost has also been seen on several occasions on horseback, galloping through the village of Lapford in Devon at the stroke of Midnight on St. John's Eve.

JEREMY BENTHAM

Famous eighteenth century eccentric, Jeremy Bentham, who died in 1832 can still be seen at University College, London. Not simply because his ghost roams around the college tapping his stick to signify his approach, but also because his mummified body dressed in his own clothes is still preserved in a glass case. His ghost visits the body occasionally to make sure that he is still there!

EMILY BRONTË

Emily Brontë lived in the heart of the bleak Yorkshire Moors in a little village called Howarth. She would wander the moors for hours alone, and eventually wrote a novel called '*Wuthering Heights*' in which Catherine Earnshaw's ghost roamed the moors searching for the man she loved, Heathcliff. Like the heroine of her novel, Emily's own ghost can now be seen walking a narrow path which leads to a waterfall on the moors, her favourite spot in life.

RUPERT BROOKE

The famous English poet, Rupert Brooke, who died during the First World War is said to haunt the Old Vicarage at Grantchester. A house which he loved and once wrote a poem about. His footsteps can now be heard walking through the garden and the house.

OLIVER CROMWELL

The ghostly spectre of Oliver Cromwell appears in numerous places throughout England. Most notably at Apsley House in London where his ghostly figure has been seen dressed in armour, particularly at times of political crisis. Cromwell and his men frequently used to hold secret meetings at the Golden Lion Inn at St. Ives in Cambridgeshire, and the figure that now haunts room 13 wearing Cromwellian dress is thought to be that of Cromwell himself. His ghost also walks through Red Lion Square in London where his exhumed body was taken on its way to Tyburn and hung **after** his death.

MARY ANNE COTTON

Notorious nineteenth century murderess who poisoned nearly twenty people, including one of her four husbands and all her four children, was executed for murder in March 1873. In recent years her ghost has been seen in the graveyard at West Auckland, County Durham, where the bodies of her victims are buried.

GRACE DARLING

This famous heroine who saved nine men who were shipwrecked off Longstone during a fierce storm in 1838, now haunts Longstone Lighthouse on Farne Islands, Northumberland, where she was born. The lighthouse keepers today seem quite happy to live with Grace Darling's ghost.

CHARLES DICKENS

Before he died, the writer Charles Dickens expressed a wish to be buried in the old burial ground of Rochester Castle in Kent. This wish was not carried out, and since his death in 1870 there have been numerous sightings of a bearded, top-hatted ghost walking round the Castle and through the burial ground. It is thought to be that of Charles Dickens. He also haunts his former home at 48 Doughty Street in London.

BENJAMIN DISRAELI

The favourite Prime Minister of Queen Victoria, Benjamin Disraeli, lived for over forty years at

Hughenden Manor in Buckinghamshire and his ghost now walks the upper floors. On several occasions he has also been seen on the steps leading from the cellar. Hughenden now belongs to the National Trust and is open to the public. Much of the house, including his study, has been left as it was when he died in 1881.

SIR FRANCIS DRAKE

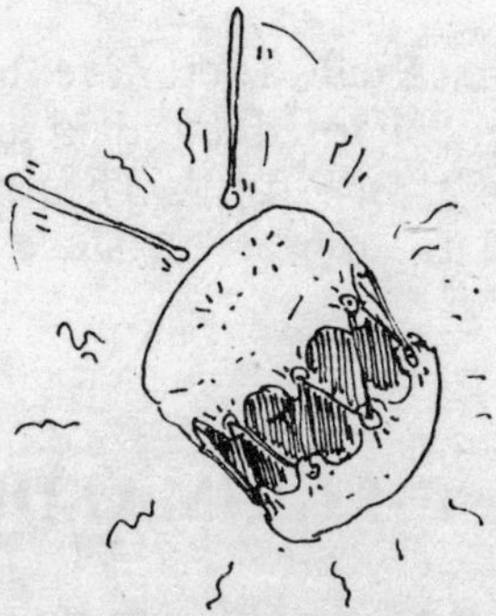

Drake's ghost frequently appears on Dartmoor on the road between Plymouth and Tavistock, usually in a black hearse-like coach pulled by headless horses and with a pack of spectral hounds running along beside. The baying of these hounds is said to be fatal to any dog that hears it. More famous still is Drake's Drum which is said to roll unaided if England is in danger. It was heard during World War I. It is said to be a sign that Drake is prepared to return to protect his country.

GUY FAWKES

Surprising though it may seem, this notorious gun-powder plotter does not wander through the cellars of the Houses of Parliament in a vain attempt to blow them up! Instead it is the ghost of a young Guy Fawkes who haunts the lanes and pathways of the Yorkshire village of Nidderdale where he spent his teenage years.

SIR HENRY IRVING

The first English actor ever to be knighted, Sir Henry Irving, collapsed and died in the middle of a performance at Bradford's Theatre Royal. His ghost continued to appear on stage until the theatre sadly closed.

JOSEPH GRIMALDI

The most famous pantomime clown of all haunts two of the most famous London theatres where he used to appear, Drury Lane and Sadlers Wells. Drury Lane is where Joey Grimaldi made his first and last appearances as a clown, and his presence can often be felt, expecially by young actors appearing there for the first time. At Sadlers Wells he has been seen sitting in one of the boxes, wearing his familiar white clown make-up.

LADY JANE GREY

The luckless Lady Jane Grey had her head chopped off on Tower Green at the Tower of London, on 12 February 1554, having been Queen of England for just nine days. Her ghostly apparition appears all in white on the anniversary of her execution. The site on which the block stood can still be seen on Tower Green.

LAWRENCE OF ARABIA

A small white-washed cottage at Cloud's Hill in Dorset, once the home of the English soldier and scholar T.E. Lawrence, is now haunted by his spectre in Arab dress. He led the Arab revolt against the Turks in 1917, and it is said by many that Lawrence always returns when Britain is in danger. Lawrence also rode a Brough Superior motor-bike and the sounds of such a bike being kick-started have often rung out through the stillness of the night.

DAN LENO

Popular Victorian comedian and pantomime dame, Dan Leno, is said to haunt the Theatre Royal at Drury Lane. Actors who have used Leno's favourite dressing room have often seen the phantom face of Dan Leno looking back at them in the make-up mirror.

IVOR NOVELLO

English composer, songwriter and actor, author of such songs as '*We'll Gather Lilacs*' and '*Keep The*

Home Fires Burning' now haunts the theatres in London where he had his greatest successes. He has been seen in the dress circle of the Palace Theatre, and in the dressing room of the Adelphi Theatre, where one of his most popular shows '*The Dancing Years*' was performed.

ALEXANDER POPE

Pope died in 1744 and remained at rest for almost a century until 1830 when someone stole his skull from his coffin, buried in St. Mary's Churchyard, Twickenham. Since that time, Pope's ghost has been seen **and heard**, dragging his crippled leg behind him. . . . . presumably still searching for his head.

DICK TURPIN

Highwayman Dick Turpin travelled the length and breadth of England during his life, which is probably why he and his phantom mare, Black Bess, are known to haunt so many different places. He haunts the George Inn, Huntingdon, where his hat and cloak still hang; Three Tuns Inn, Cambridge; the Rose and Crown, Hempstead; his former home, Turpin's House, Thaxted; Epping Forest where his hideout used to be; the Debtor's Prison, York (where the bed on which he spent his last night can still be seen); and the Knavesmire in York where he was hanged on the gallows in April 1739. Three times a year Turpin's ghost gallops down Trapp's Hill, near Loughton, Essex, and has been seen many times in Bury Lane, Bedfordshire. It is also thought that the '*gentleman in green velvet*' who haunts the Chequers in Bickley, Kent, could also be our much travelled highwayman for it was here that Turpin had a secret escape route via some backstairs to the bedroom in which he hid.

SIR WALTER RALEIGH

On St. Michael's Eve (29 September) the spectre of Sir Walter Raleigh walks through the grounds of Sherborne Castle, which he built, and can occasionally be seen sitting underneath a tree which bears his name. Unlike many ghosts, it is not thought that Raleigh haunts the spot where he was buried (although nobody knows exactly where it is.) After his execution, his wife carried the embalmed severed head around with her in her handbag. The head is now buried at West Horsley, and his heart is buried at Old Carew House, Beddington, Surrey. Sir Walter has often been seen at Beddington, where he often used to visit with Queen Elizabeth I.

SIR CHRISTOPHER WREN

Architect and builder of St. Paul's Cathedral, and over fifty of London's other churches, Sir Christopher is said to walk through his former home, the Old Court House, Hampton Court, on the anniversary of his death, 26 February. Indeed, on this night ghostly footsteps have been heard . . .

X Marks The Spot

Surprisingly, ghosts very rarely haunt graveyards but instead linger in the places where they once lived, or indeed on the spot where they died. On such spots strange reminders of what happened remain forever. . . .

ACLE BRIDGE, Norfolk.

Josiah Burge was a murderer. He murdered a woman, whose brother in turn murdered Burge on Acle Bridge. One year later a ghostly skeleton murdered the brother. Every year on 7th April fresh blood appears on Acle Bridge at the spot where Josiah Burge was killed.

BOSWORTH HALL, Leicestershire.

During the time of the Roundheads a monk hid at Bosworth Hall, knowing that he would be murdered if he was discovered. When the Roundheads came in search for him the monk ran to a secret hideout, knocking over the Communion wine as he did so. The red stain still remains, and is **still** damp after three hundred years. Some say that it isn't wine at all, but the monk's blood.

BLOODY CORNER, Dartmoor.

At the village of Drewsteignton there is a cottage at a place now known as Bloody Corner. In this cottage someone was murdered centuries ago, but a trickle of blood still seeps out from under the cottage door to mark the spot where the murder took place.

CLIFFSEND, Kent.

There once stood a gibbet in Cliffsend where criminals met their deaths, and were buried close by. This eerie spot is haunted by their lost souls and several strange accidents have happened to people near this place.

DAVIES GRAVE, Montgomery.

In 1821 William Davies, a highwayman, was hanged for a murder that he did not commit. Before he was executed he claimed that no grass would ever grow on his grave, and at the moment of his death a violent thunderstorm started. Although many people have tried to grow grass on his grave, to this very day a small cross of barren ground appears on his grave.

THE FOOTPRINT

In 1684 young William Batt of Oakwell Hall in Birstall, West Yorkshire, set out on a journey to London — which in those days took a very long time. He was supposed to return on Christmas Eve, but his family were very surprised when on the 22nd December they saw William enter the house and climb the stairs. When they went to look for him, he wasn't there. They would have thought it just a dream, had they not discovered on the stairs a footprint in **wet blood**. The next day news reached them that William had been murdered in London. On the anniversary of his death it is said that the footprint appears again, still wet.

THE GREAT HOUSE

At Cheshunt, Hertfordshire, there is a house known as the Great House which is haunted by a grey lady. She is said to have been murdered in the house, and in one of the bedrooms there is a blood stain that no amount of scrubbing can remove.

TRAIL OF BLOOD

An old Yorkshire shopkeeper, with the marvellous name of Leathery Coit, used to keep his horse, on which he travelled through the moors selling his wares, at the Fleece Inn at Elland. One night, for a reason we shall never know, old Leathery was murdered at the Inn. As the murderer dragged his body down the stairs a trail of blood was left behind. The stain remains and nothing will remove it.

Year of Ghosts

If you want to be a ghost hunter, here is a list of ghosts who are said to appear regularly every year. These are the places to be, or perhaps the places to avoid!

JANUARY

1st

At midnight Lady Howard's ghost drives along the Okehampton-Tavistock road in Devon. She rides in a coach made of bones, driven by a headless coachman and pulled by headless horses.

4th

A phantom dog, known as the 'Hound of Ill-Omen' appears on the road between Knockandhu and Milton of Auchriachan, Nairnshire, Scotland. If there is snow on the ground it leaves tracks larger than a man's hand.

6th

At Langley Hall, County Durham, a phantom hearse pulled by headless horses appears at midnight.

30th

John Bradshaw, who signed Charles I's death warrant, can be seen and heard in the passage outside the Inslip Rooms of the Deanery at Westminster Abbey.

FEBRUARY

2nd

At Bealings House, Ipswich, unseen hands cause bells to ring.

3rd

The road at St. Blazey, Cornwall, is haunted by a strange creature that looks like a bear, but makes a sound like a horse.

12th

Lady Jane Grey haunts the Tower of London on the anniversary of her death.

13th

Six kilometres off Goodwin Sands a ghostly ship, the '*Lady Luvibund*' appears. It was sunk in 1748.

26th

The wraith of Sir Christopher Wren haunts his former home, '*Old Court House*', Hampton Court, on the anniversary of his death.

MARCH

9th

Cavalier, Lord Capel, haunts his home 'Cassiobury' in Watford on the anniversary of his execution 1649.

11th

The last highwayman to be hanged, Robert Snooks, haunts his grave on Boxmoor Common.

15th

Bishop Thomas Ken visits the library named after him at Longleat House, Wiltshire.

16th

The ghost of Lord Stourton (hanged 1557) walks through Salisbury Cathedral.

17th

St. Juliet's Eve. The ghost of a girl appears at midnight at the Ferryboat Inn, Holywell, Huntingdon.

24th

Queen Elizabeth I appears at the gatehouse of Richmond Palace. The place where her ring was thrown to a rider to take to James IV of Scotland as proof that she was dead and that he was King of England.

25th

William Hunter haunts 'The Swan Inn', Brentwood, Essex, where he spent his last night before being burned at the stake in 1555.

30th

John Massey, a wrestler who murdered his wife in 1801, was hanged at the gallows on Red Hill, Bilstone, Warwickshire. On this night his ghost appears at the gibbet.

APRIL

7th

Fresh blood appears on the bridge at Acle, Norfolk, which is haunted by murderer, Josiah Burge. Also the ghost of Margaret Reay, shot in 1779, appears at Admiralty House, London.

8th

A ghostly fiddler plays at Binham, Norfolk.

10th

Margaret Gould haunts Lewtrenchard House, Devon.

13th

A ghostly Roman procession of horses and chariots sets out from Wroxham to travel to Brancaster in Norfolk.

26th

The spectre of Kate Penfound appears at Penfound Manor in Cornwall.

MAY

1st

If you have a stiff neck, go to Launceston Churchyard on 1st, 2nd or 3rd May and pass your hands over the grave of the last person to have been buried there.

13th

Highwayman, Jack Diamond, haunts his cottage in West Peckham, Kent, at 6.30 pm at the time of his death.

19th

Anne Boleyn's headless ghost appears at Blickling Hall, Norfolk.

25th

A ghostly monk walks through St. Benet's, Norfolk.

30th

Wraith of a Miss Wallis is said to appear in Union Street, Aberdeen.

31st

At Potter Heigham, Norfolk, a phantom coach with skeleton driver carries off Lady Carew, screaming.

JUNE

7th

On this day in 1679 Sarah Fletcher hanged herself at Clifton Hawden, Oxfordshire. Her ghost remains there still.

15th

A grey lady haunts Hitchin Priory, Hertfordshire.

JULY

3rd

On this night a ghostly body wrapped in a white shroud appears to be thrown from Burgh Castle, Norfolk.

15th

James, Duke of Monmouth, haunts Sedgemoor, Somerset, where he was beheaded, 1685.

18th

The ghost of a nun walks through Exeter Cathedral, 7pm.

20th

Every five years on this night a ghostly coronation takes place in Horning, Norfolk.

21st

Spectral hounds can be heard howling on Purse Caundle bowling green, Somerset.

25th

A ghostly ship sails into St. Ives Head harbour. If anyone tries to board it, it disappears.

AUGUST

2nd

On the anniversary of his death in 1100 King William Rufus follows the route that his body was taken on its final journey to Winchester.

22nd

The headless ghost of Sir John Gates appears at Beeleigh Abbey, Maldon, Essex.

SEPTEMBER

2nd

Dame Alice Lisle appears at the Eclipse Inn, Winchester, where she spent her last night before being beheaded.

29th

Sir Walter Raleigh's ghost strolls through Sherbourne Castle, Somerset.

OCTOBER

7th – 9th

Ghostly procession of Roman chariots that set out on 13th April arrives in Branchester, Norfolk.

10th

An unknown lady from the Scalmers family haunts the churchyard of Mannington Hall, Norfolk, apparently searching for her tomb, now destroyed.

18th

Ghostly music and rattling chains heard at Hastings castle.

25th

King George II's ghost haunts Kensington Palace on the anniversary of his death.

NOVEMBER

3rd

Lady Coleraine's ghost appears screaming on the balcony of Bruce Castle, London, now the Tottenham Museum.

4th

Dame Dorothy Selby haunts Igtham Mote, Kent, pleading with Lord Monteagle to keep away from the Houses of Parliament on 5th November 1605.

5th

At Shebbear, North Devon, bell ringers ring the bells to frighten away the devil, and turn the Devil's Stone in the churchyard.

30th

At Tavistock Place, Bloomsbury, the ghost of a nurse approaches a man in mourning, then turns away and vanishes.

DECEMBER

7th

Actor, William Terriss, haunts the Adelphi Theatre (London) stagedoor where he was murdered, 1897.

16th

The Brown Lady walks through Raynham Hall, Norfolk. Witnesses say her eye-sockets are empty.

20th

Path from Neville's Cross to Cradlewell, County Durham, is haunted by the ghost of a murdered woman with a child by her side.

22nd

Phantom of a hanged man swings from an oak tree, 2.45 pm at Stocken House, Stretton, Rutland.

23rd

Queen Elizabeth I haunts library at Windsor Castle.

24th

King Arthur and his knights ride out from Cadbury Castle. A phantom Roman chariot drives through Black Greve Farm, Wythall, at midnight.

27th

St. John's Eve. St. Thomas of Canterbury gallops through Lapford, South Devon, at midnight.

28th

Anne Boleyn's headless ghost haunts Rochford Hall, Essex.

31st

Colonel Thomas Sydney appears at Ranworth Broad, Norfolk, on the anniversary of his murder, 1770.

Zzzzzz

If you're reading this book in bed, don't be frightened by ghosts — have a laugh before you go to sleep! Here are some frightfully funny jokes, about everything other than ghosts!

'Waiter, waiter, I've only got one piece of meat.'
'Alright, I'll cut it in two for you.'

'So you're not going to Paris this year then?'
'No, it's Egypt we're not going to this year. It was Paris we didn't go to last year.'

'I say waiter, there are seven flies in my soup!'
'What a pity — just one more and you would have had a world record.'

Where does a goose come from?

A gooseberry bush.

What does the sea say to the sand?

Nothing, it just waves.

PATIENT: After hearing what you've said, I want a second opinion.
DOCTOR: OK, you've had my first opinion. My second opinion is that there is still nothing wrong with you.

What did the housewife say to the plumber when he had finished mending her cistern?

Tanks very much.

TEACHER: What does it mean when the barometer falls?
CYNTHIA: The nail's come out of the wall, miss.

What is the best place for a party on a ship?

Where the funnel be.

A jeweller was standing in his shop when suddenly a man came flying through the window.
'What on earth is going on?' asked the jeweller.
'I forgot to let go of the brick,' said the man.

What happened to the boy who slept with his head under a pillow?

When he woke up the fairies had taken all his teeth out.

How do you define '**Agony**'?

A man with one arm hanging from a cliff-top when his nose itches.

What's the difference between a square peg in a round whole and half a ton of lard?

One's a fat lot of good, the other's a good lot of fat.

What would you eat on board ship during a storm?

The cheapest thing on the menu.

MOTHER: I've made the chicken soup.
BOY: Thank heaven's for that, I thought it was for us.

FATHER: It looks like rain again.
MOTHER: Well, it said chicken soup on the packet.

DRIVING INSTRUCTOR: I think you'd better slow down.
LEARNER: But I'm allowed to do forty miles an hour in this area.
DRIVING INSTRUCTOR: Not on the pavement though.

OLD LADY: Could you see me across the road?
BOY SCOUT: I don't know, I'll go over and have a look.

What did Lady Hamilton say to Nelson?

You're the one-eye care for.

Did you hear the story about the empty box?
There was nothing in it.

BOSS: So you want a job do you?
APPLICANT: Yes, sir.
BOSS: What's your name?
APPLICANT: Charlie Chaplin.
BOSS: That's a very well known name.
APPLICANT: It ought to be, I've been delivering papers around here for years.

'I want a hair-cut please.'
'Certainly, sir. Which one?'

TEACHER: Who was the very first woman?
KAREN: I don't know, miss.
TEACHER: Come on, Karen. It was something to do with an apple. . . .
KAREN: Oh, I know! Granny Smith.

What's black and white and bounces?

A rubber nun.

What do misers do when it's cold?

Sit round a candle.

What do misers do when it's very cold?

Light it.

Why did the hedgehog cross the road?

To see his flatmate.

Why did the one-eyed chicken cross the road?

To get to the Bird's Eye shop.

'Doctor, doctor, I've only got 59 seconds left to live.'
'Wait a minute, please.'

'My grandma is incredible, she's ninety-four and not a grey hair on her head. She's completely bald.'

What is Dracula's favourite slogan?

Please give blood generously.

What did one piano say to the other piano?
'You may consider yourself grand, but at least I'm upright.'

What is the best way for a ghost-hunter to keep fit?
He must exorcise regularly.

'What's that horrible ugly thing on your shoulder?'
'I don't know — what?'
'YOUR HEAD!'

CHALLENGE BY GYLES BRANDRETH

Can YOU eat a bowl of soup with a fork?
Can YOU blow a bubble to beat the world bubble gum record?
Can YOU put on every single pair of socks you own – one after the other?
Can YOU do up your buttons, peel a banana and comb your hair without using your thumbs?

Challenges for journeys, challenges for rainy days, challenges alone and challenges with friends – treasure hunts, brain busters, puzzles, tricks and daredevil dares – can you take a CHALLENGE???

ISBN 0 552 54194 X 85p

WHAT DO YOU KNOW? BY GYLES BRANDRETH

What do you know about *your* body, *your* family, *your* school, *your* neighbourhood, the world, entertainment, sport, wildlife, the stars and planets and much, much more?

Fill in your information in the sections provided for an extraordinary and unique, personal encyclopaedia of your very own life and store of knowledge, recorded for all time!!!

ISBN 0 552 54233 4 95p

PRINCE PHILIP PRESENTS 101 GREAT GAMES

BY PETER HESELTINE AND PAUL JAMES

Games to play indoors; games to play outdoors; games to play on your own and games to play with friends. Some are traditional games, some are new games – but they will all give you hours of fun and pleasure.

ISBN 0 552 54246 6 £1.25

If you would like to receive a newsletter telling you about our new children's books, fill in the coupon with your name and address and send it to:

Ingrid Selberg
Transworld Publishers Ltd.,
Century House,
61–63 Uxbridge Road, Ealing,
London, W5 5SA

Name ....

Address ....

....

....

CHILDREN'S NEWSLETTER

All the books on the previous pages are available at your bookshop or can be ordered direct from Transworld Publishers Ltd., Cash Sales Dept., P.O. Box 11, Falmouth, Cornwall.
Please send full name and address together with cheque or postal order — no currency, and allow 22p per book to cover postage and packing (plus 10 p each for additional copies).